THE NEW FINANCE

OVERREACTION, COMPLEXITY, AND THEIR CONSEQUENCES

The Prentice Hall Series in Finance

Alexander/Sharpe/Bailey
Fundamentals of Investments

Bear/Moldonado-Bear
Free Markets, Finance, Ethics, and Law

Berk/DeMarzo
*Corporate Finance**

Berk/DeMarzo
*Corporate Finance: The Core**

Berk/DeMarzo/Harford
*Fundamentals of Corporate Finance**

Bierman/Smidt
The Capital Budgeting Decision: Economic Analysis of Investment Projects

Bodie/Merton/Cleeton
Financial Economics

Click/Coval
The Theory and Practice of International Financial Management

Copeland/Weston/Shastri
Financial Theory and Corporate Policy

Cox/Rubinstein
Options Markets

Dorfman
Introduction to Risk Management and Insurance

Dietrich
Financial Services and Financial Institutions: Value Creation in Theory and Practice

Dufey/Giddy
Cases in International Finance

Eakins
Finance in learn

Eiteman/Stonehill/Moffett
Multinational Business Finance

Emery/Finnerty/Stowe
Corporate Financial Management

Fabozzi
Bond Markets: Analysis and Strategies

Fabozzi/Modigliani
Capital Markets: Institutions and Instruments

Fabozzi/Modigliani/Jones
Foundations of Financial Markets and Institutions

Finkler
Financial Management for Public, Health, and Not-for-Profit Organizations

Francis/Ibbotson
Investments: A Global Perspective

Frasca
Personal Finance: An Integrated Planning Approach

Fraser/Ormiston
Understanding Financial Statements

Geisst
Investment Banking in the Financial System

Gitman
*Principles of Managerial Finance**

Gitman
*Principles of Managerial Finance—Brief Edition**

Gitman/Joehnk
*Fundamentals of Investing**

Gitman/Madura
Introduction to Finance

Guthrie/Lemon
Mathematics of Interest Rates and Finance

Haugen
The Inefficient Stock Market: What Pays Off and Why

Haugen
Modern Investment Theory

Haugen
The New Finance: Overreaction, Complexity, and Uniqueness

Holden
Excel Modeling and Estimation in the Fundamentals of Corporate Finance

Holden
Excel Modeling and Estimation in the Fundamentals of Investments

Holden
Excel Modeling and Estimation in Investments

Holden
Excel Modeling and Estimation in Corporate Finance

Hughes/MacDonald
International Banking: Text and Cases

Hull
Fundamentals of Futures and Options Markets

Hull
Options, Futures, and Other Derivatives

Hull
Risk Management and Financial Institutions

Keown/Martin/Petty/Scott
Financial Management: Principles and Applications

Keown/Martin/Petty/Scott
Foundations of Finance: The Logic and Practice of Financial Management

Keown
Personal Finance: Turning Money into Wealth

Kim/Nofsinger
Corporate Governance

Levy/Post
Investments

May/May/Andrew
Effective Writing: A Handbook for Finance People

Madura
Personal Finance

Marthinsen
Risk Takers: Uses and Abuses of Financial Derivatives

McDonald
Derivatives Markets

McDonald
Fundamentals of Derivatives Markets

Megginson
Corporate Finance Theory

Melvin
International Money and Finance

Mishkin/Eakins
Financial Markets and Institutions

Moffett
Cases in International Finance

Moffett/Stonehill/Eiteman
Fundamentals of Multinational Finance

Nofsinger
Psychology of Investing

Ogden/Jen/O'Connor
Advanced Corporate Finance

Pennacchi
Theory of Asset Pricing

Rejda
Principles of Risk Management and Insurance

Schoenebeck
Interpreting and Analyzing Financial Statements

Scott/Martin/Petty/Keown/Thatcher
Cases in Finance

Seiler
Performing Financial Studies: A Methodological Cookbook

Shapiro
Capital Budgeting and Investment Analysis

Sharpe/Alexander/Bailey
Investments

Solnik/McLeavey
Global Investments

Stretcher/Michael
Cases in Financial Management

Titman/Martin
Valuation: The Art and Science of Corporate Investment Decisions

Trivoli
Personal Portfolio Management: Fundamentals and Strategies

Van Horne
Financial Management and Policy

Van Horne
Financial Market Rates and Flows

Van Horne/Wachowicz
Fundamentals of Financial Management

Vaughn
Financial Planning for the Entrepreneur

Weston/Mitchel/Mulherin
Takeovers, Restructuring, and Corporate Governance

*denotes  titles. Log onto www.myfinancelab.com to learn more

FOURTH EDITION

THE NEW FINANCE

OVERREACTION, COMPLEXITY, AND THEIR CONSEQUENCES

Robert A. Haugen

President, Haugen Custom Financial Systems

Prentice Hall

Boston   Columbus   Indianapolis   New York
San Francisco   Upper Saddle River_Amsterdam   Cape Town
Dubai   London   Madrid   Milan   Munich   Paris   Montreal   Toronto_Delhi
Mexico City   Sao Paulo   Sydney   Hong Kong   Seoul   Singapore   Taipei   Tokyo

Editor in Chief: Donna Battista
Assistant Editor: Mary Kate Murray
Managing Editor: Jeff Holcomb
Production Manager: Kathleen Sleys
Media Project Manager: Holly Wallace
Marketing Assistant: Ian Gold

Rights and Permissions Advisor: Charles Morris
Art Director: Jayne Conte
Project Management, Composition, and Illustrations: Integra Software Services, Ltd.
Cover Image: © Getty Images
Cover Design: Bruce Kenselaar

Library of Congress Cataloging-in-Publication Data
Haugen, Robert A.
    The new finance: overreaction, complexity, and their consequences / Robert A. Haugen.—4th ed.
        p. cm.
    ISBN-13: 978-0-13-603604-3 (alk. paper)
    ISBN-10: 0-13-603604-X (alk. paper)
    1. Efficient market theory.   2. Stocks—Prices—United States.   3. Capital
market—United States.   I. Title.
HG4915.H383 2010
332—dc22

                                                                                2009007230

1 2 3 4 5 6 7 8 9 10—CRS—14 13 12 11 10 09

Prentice Hall
is an imprint of

www.pearsonhighered.com

ISBN-13: 978-0-13-603604-3
ISBN-10:   0-13-603604-X

Dedicated to Jan Bowler and Jack Daulton,
my pupils and teachers
For what is likely to be my final words on these issues go to
http://ssrn.com/abstract=1306523

Additional Prentice Hall Titles by Robert Haugen

Modern Investment Theory, Fifth Edition (2000)

Beast on Wall Street (1999)

The Inefficient Stock Market, Second Edition (2001)

Visit Robert Haugen's Web site at:

http://www.quantitativeinvestment.com

CONTENTS

PREFACE

This work makes the case for an *inefficient* stock market, where the complexity and uniqueness of investor interactions has important market pricing consequences.

The efficient market's paradigm is at the unlikely extreme end of a spectrum of possible states. As such, the burden of proof falls on its advocates. It is their burden to deflect the stones and arrows flung at the paradigm by the nonbelievers. It is their burden to reveal the inaccuracies of those who present evidence contending that the paradigm doesn't square with the facts.

Moreover, the case of market *efficiency* has been made many times by others.[1] In fairness to the growing number of advocates for the *other side*, I present here, and in the two other books of this trilogy, *Beast on Wall Street: How Stock Volatility Devours Our Wealth* and *The Inefficient Stock Market: What Pays Off and Why*, a comprehensive and organized collection of the evidence and the arguments that constitute a strong and persuasive case for a complex and, at times, nearly chaotic stock market that *overreacts* to most things—in particular, to past records of success and failure on the part of business firms. It is a market that prices with great *imprecision*, with signals coming from the prices of other stocks as its *dominant driver*.

In the course of this work, I shall make a case for the following assertions:

- Players in today's stock market persistently make a fundamental mistake—overreacting to records of success and failure on the part of business firms. This mistake was also made in the distant past, only to be rectified. Stock investors began making the mistake once again in the late 1950s, and they continue to make it today. Those who recognize the mistake can build stock portfolios, or find mutual funds, that will subsequently outperform the market averages.
- Owing to the foregoing mistake, the stocks that can be expected to produce the highest returns in the future are the safest stocks. Risky stocks can be expected to produce the lowest returns!
- Because of agency problems in the investment business, the opportunity that is there *now* is likely to *remain* there in the future.
- Models in financial economics aggregate from assumed preferences to conclusions about market pricing. Game-theoretic models consider interactions among market participants, but given the preferences, wealth, information, and other aspects explicitly considered, responses to identical stimuli are presumed to be identical. *The New Finance* argues that each interaction must be considered as entirely *unique*, making aggregation, in any way, from the preferences and behaviors of interacting individuals to meaningful conclusions about the structure and behavior of market prices a meaningless exercise. Thus, both rational and behavioral economics need to be reconsidered.
- Investor interaction creates an additional component of volatility in stock return. Explosions in this price-driven component of volatility were responsible for the Great Crash of 1929 and the Great Depression.

[1] See, for example, E. Fama, "Efficient Markets II," *Journal of Finance* (December 1991).

NEW TO THIS EDITION

The best and most important work of my career appears in the following two new chapters. Chapter 10, "The Real Determinants of Expected Stock Returns," discusses expected return factor models. This new study (never published before) shows the historic performance of three models (by decade) from 1962 to the present. This chapter also shows a remarkable consistency in the determinants of expected stock returns—decade by decade. Chapter 11, "Dangerous Conversation," which is highly relevant to the current financial crisis, discusses evidence on the nature of stock volatility, as well as the historic relationship between the stock market and economic activity.

Throughout the book, charts and tables were updated and recently published studies were added as appropriate to the content of each chapter. This edition of the book was written and submitted for publication during the summer of 2008. By the time it was returned to me for copy editing in January, 2009, the global economic landscape had changed dramatically. I think you'll find Chapter 11 particularly relevant to our current conditions. Now I, like you, am left to hope that stock volatility subsides and we avert an economic disaster.

ACKNOWLEDGMENTS

I wish to gratefully acknowledge the research assistance of Jan Bowler, Tom Fees, and Fred Elbert.

R.A.H.

ABOUT THE AUTHOR

Robert Haugen has held endowed chairs at the University of Wisconsin, the University of Illinois, and the University of California. He is the author of more than 50 articles in leading finance journals and 15 books, which have collectively been published in seven languages. These include: *The Incredible January Effect*, *Beast on Wall Street*, and *The Inefficient Stock Market*. He is President of Haugen Custom Financial Systems, which licenses the output of an expected return factor model to pension funds, endowments, institutional, and high-net-worth money managers.

CHAPTER 1

Search for the Grail

THE SEARCHERS

For decades, finance professors in business schools worldwide have continued to tenaciously sift through computerized data files. These files contain information on security prices and accounting numbers. The professors have been in search of patterns and clues about why the market behaves as it does.

In the last three decades, this search for the way the stock market works has paid off. The secrets of the market's behavior—the proverbial Holy Grail to stock investors—are rapidly unfolding.

The results fly directly in the face of the existing financial economic paradigm—what is called *Modern Finance*—the collection of wisdom that every MBA is required to master. Evidence supporting this conventional thinking has been diminishing. Instead we now see a market that is highly imprecise and mostly overreactive in its pricing; a market literally turned upside down—where the highest-risk stocks can be expected to produce the lowest returns and the lowest-risk stocks, the highest returns!

What we are seeing is so profound that it is nothing short of the beginning of a paradigm shift. Modern Finance may be displaced by something I call the *New Finance*. Substantiation is unfolding about what stocks are best to invest in, how firms should raise capital, how utilities should be regulated, and how CFOs should estimate their cost of capital.

Overwhelming evidence is piling up that investors overreact to the past performance of firms, pricing **growth stocks** (stocks that sell at above-average prices relative to current cash flows, earnings, dividends, and book values) too high relative to these numbers and **value stocks** (stocks that sell at below average prices) too low relative to their numbers. Subsequent to these overreactions, over the long run, the expensive stocks produce low returns for the investors who buy them at high prices, and, similarly, the cheap stocks produce high returns for their investors.

THE CELEBRATED F&F STUDY

Although studies documenting the relative performance of value and growth stocks have been in print for years, they were mostly ignored by the proponents of Modern Finance. These studies were dismissed because they allegedly had problems that made their findings suspect.

For example, some had survival bias. They examined only the performance of value and growth stocks that managed to survive for the entire period of the study. Since value stocks tend to have relatively poor prospects, it is fair to say that of the stocks that fail to survive, many may be value stocks than growth. Leaving the non-survivors out can create a misleading picture of their true realized relative performance.

But some of the dismissed studies were pretty much free of bias problems.

But then why were they dismissed?

As you read through this book, keep asking yourself that question.

In any case, everything changed with the publication of the results of a now classic study by two professors from the University of Chicago, Eugene Fama and Ken French (F&F).[1] Fama was the original champion of the notion that the stock market is efficient. In an efficient market, any differences in the performance between value and growth must be due to the fact that value stocks are more risky. That is what F&F claimed in their article. F&F offered no proof to support their contention, and they provide (although they don't discuss it) evidence that the very opposite is true.

Not only was the F&F study not ignored, but it was also voted the best article published in the *Journal of Finance* in 1992 by the widest margin in history. The *Journal of Finance* is the oldest and most prestigious journal in academic finance.

The F&F study spans the period running from the early 1960s through 1990, and it covers nearly all stocks traded on the New York Stock Exchange (NYSE), the American Stock Exchange (AMEX), and the over-the-counter market, the National Association of Securities Dealers Automated Quotations (NASDAQ).

F&F focus on the relationship between the accounting value of stockholders' equity, the *book value*, and the *market value* of their stock.

Book value is the accountant's estimate of the value of a stockholder's stake in the firm. To a great extent, it is based on historical cost. You start with the accounting value of the total assets of the firm and then subtract the claims on the assets that come ahead of the stockholders'. These claims would include amounts owed to suppliers, to the bank, to bondholders, and others. What's left is for the stockholders.

As stated earlier, to a large extent, book value is based on historical costs—it doesn't reflect the value of future prospects.

Conversely, the market value of the stock *does* reflect these prospects. If the prospects of future growth are better than average, the market value will be large relative to the book value.

Think of a company that has recently introduced a new and exciting product. The historical cost of its assets in place may be small, but sales and earnings are up, and the firm has great prospects for generating even greater cash flow in the future. The market has valued the stock of this company highly. The book value of this growth stock will be small now in relation to its market value. The question for the future, however, is, "Will competitors enter the market with their own versions of the product with lower prices and smaller profit margins, forcing the profitability of this firm to revert to average levels?" If the market doesn't properly discount this possibility into the *current price*, it will be unpleasantly surprised as competitors enter, the stock price falls, and *future returns* become *disappointing*.

The opposite may be true for a stock with poor growth prospects.

Think of a company that is inefficient and poorly organized. Earnings reports have been poor, and the stock price has declined, based on the assumption that the firm will continue its unprofitable ways. For this inexpensive *value* stock, book value (the historic cost of assets) is large relative to market value. Again, the question for the future is, "Will the board of directors force existing management out, bring in a fresh team to reorganize the firm, and then raise its profitability back to average levels?" If the market doesn't discount this possibility into the current price, it will be pleasantly surprised as the firm becomes more efficient, the stock price rises, and future returns become surprisingly *good*. What goes around comes around.

Perhaps you remember that some time ago, the Dallas Cowboys football team went from winning Super Bowls (expensive growth stock) to the bottom of the league (cheap value stock) and back to winning Super Bowls (expensive growth stock again) and back and forth some more.

In any case, **expensive growth stocks:** *low book-to-market*; **cheap value stocks:** *high book-to-market.*

And F&F want to know the relative magnitude of *future* returns for stocks that have *different* book-to-market ratios *now*.

They begin in mid-1963. Across the firms in their sample, they rank the stocks based on the ratio of book-to-market value.

Cheap stocks on the top; expensive stocks on the bottom.

The ranking is done at mid-year because they want to be sure that an investor who might have performed this exercise had access to both numbers (book and market) needed to compute the ratio. Although today's market value is available today, the book value isn't reported until several months after the close of the fiscal year. Presumably, by July 1 nearly all firms would have reported their book values.

Based on the rankings, the stocks are sorted into 10 groups, each containing an equal number of stocks. The least expensive stocks are in group 1 and the most expensive are in group 10.

The groups are bought and held as portfolios until mid-1964. Then the stocks that existed at that time are reranked by book-to-market value, and the portfolios are reformed in the same way that they were in 1963.

Again, they observe the performance of groups 1 through 10 through mid-1965. And the process is repeated year after year through 1990.

The average annual return (1963–90) for each of the groups is plotted in Figure 1-1.[2]

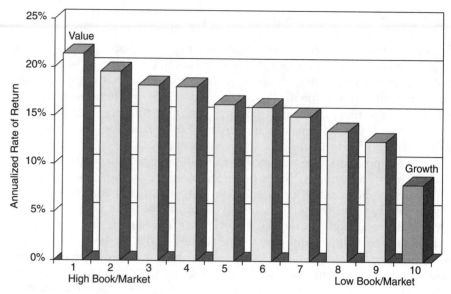

FIGURE 1-1 Book-to-Market as a Predictor of Return

Take a good look.

That's *21.4%* for the cheap stocks and only *8%* for the expensive stocks.[3]

And as we go from group 1 (cheapest), to 2, then 3, and so on, the returns keep falling.

To be sure, each of the groups contains nearly 200 stocks, and individual stocks migrate from group to group over time. Prospects change, and stocks may change from expensive to cheap and even back again. But, for well-diversified portfolios, the ratio of book/market value is an extremely good predictor of future return.

This is not to say that *all* expensive stocks are destined to produce poor future returns. In any given year, the stocks in group 10 produce returns over a very wide range.

Microsoft is probably a member of group 10. But its very high returns in this period are offset by the low returns of scores of other growth stocks with great prospects that didn't "pan out."

Diamond Head or Diamond Bar?

Now let's concentrate on the meaning of the difference between 8% and 21.4% in the context of compound interest.

Suppose you're an investor of average means, and you're able to come up with $2,000 each year to invest in an IRA. You're 30 years old, and you plan to retire at age 65.

That gives you 35 years to accumulate a nest egg.

How to invest the money?

You have a choice. You can invest in expensive growth stocks (Portfolio 10) or in cheap value stocks (Portfolio 1).

An annual return of 8% in nominal dollars is equivalent to an annual return of 2.47% *in real dollars*, given the average rate of inflation over the F&F study. This real return makes your nest egg grow to $109,232 at retirement (real dollars). If, in your golden years, you continue to invest in something that earns a 2.47% real rate of return (like expensive stocks), you will be able to draw a retirement income of $2,698 annually without eating into real principal:

$$\$109,232 \times 2.47\% = \$2,698 \text{ per year}$$

Good luck, and have a really *great* retirement!

On the other hand, if you invest in something that produces the returns that the cheapest stocks (Portfolio 1) had, your nest egg grows as in the rear bars of Figure 1-2.

With a *real* rate of return of 15.18%, by the time retirement comes, you will have accumulated $1,839,369. If you continue to invest in this way *past* retirement, you will be able to draw an annual income of $279,216 in inflation-adjusted dollars:

$$\$1,839,369 \times 15.18\% = \$279,216 \text{ per year}$$

Think of it.

For a 30-year-old investor, investing a mere $2,000 per year in an IRA, the past performance differential between cheap/value and expensive/growth stocks can mean *100 times* more wealth at retirement, the difference between retiring in *luxury* or in *poverty*. This can mean the difference between retiring at Waikiki Beach in the shadow of *Diamond Head* or in the midst of the smog-filled San Gabriel Valley in an unexciting place called *Diamond Bar*. And even to live in Diamond Bar, you're going to need some real help from your rich uncle!

You have the opportunity to *choose* between going to Diamond Head or Diamond Bar.

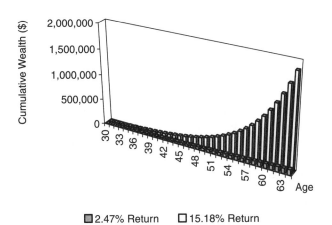

FIGURE 1-2 The Roads to Diamond Bar and Diamond Head

Will Go Go Away?

Note that the Golden Opportunity (GO) of the New Finance is a *long-term* strategy. It won't make you rich overnight, but it isn't going to vanish before our eyes either. Assuming that the economic downturn of 2008 is a historical aberration; the consensus opinion of investment experts is that *over the long term*, equities should continue to produce the kinds of returns we've always seen. And we're not likely to see massive amounts of capital move into GO, increasing its price and driving down its subsequent return.

Why? Because, as it turns out, stock prices are dominated by institutional investors (pension funds, insurance companies, trust and endowment funds). Because the fiduciaries, that run their portfolios, are subject to severe penalties for short-term underperformance, *they will be sorely afraid to take advantage of GO*.

These institutional investors are becoming increasingly aware of GO, but it's an opportunity they're very reluctant to take advantage of. The performance of the directors of these funds is evaluated over periods of three to five years. So, the directors themselves have very short horizons.[4] For stock investments, performance is usually measured relative to a stock index called the S&P 500. This index roughly contains the largest 500 stocks in the United States. As we shall show later, in terms of total market capitalization (price per share times number of shares outstanding), it contains much more growth than value.

The performance of the S&P 500 is dominated by expensive growth stocks.

Because these fiduciaries are likely to be *fired* if their stock investments fall short of the S&P 500 *in the short term*, they are sorely afraid to shun expensive growth for cheap value, even though they know this brings superior performance *in the long term*.

That leaves GO for us—the lowly individual investor. If the institutions stay put, and it is likely that they will, GO will remain available to us. If it continues to be, you won't need a lot of capital to get rich in the stock market.

Two thousand dollars per year can take you to Diamond Head.

LOW RISK, HIGH RETURN?

More good news. The road to Diamond Head is less bumpy than the road to Diamond Bar because you get to Diamond Head by investing in relatively *safe* stocks.

As it turns out, expensive stocks are riskier than cheap stocks. Stock portfolios that contain large numbers of expensive stocks have returns that are more variable from year to year. Much is expected from them, and the market is often unpleasantly surprised. Less is expected out of cheap stocks (much fewer unpleasant surprises) and, as a consequence, their periodic returns are much more stable.

Back to the F&F study.

We can use the results of F&F to find out if growth stocks are really riskier.

   F&F measure risk by something called beta. Beta tells us the sensitivity of a stock's returns to changes in the return to the market index (S&P 500). Suppose a stock has a beta of 1/2. This means that if the return to the S&P were to go up by 1%, we would expect the stock's returns to go up by 0.5%. On the other hand, if the stock had a beta of 2.00, its return would be expected to go up by 2%, or twice the increase in return on the S&P.

   Beta, as it turns out, is proportional to the contribution that an individual stock makes to the risk, or volatility of return, of the stock portfolio that it's computed with respect to. For example, if a stock has a beta of 2.00 against the S&P 500, the stock's contribution to the volatility of the S&P is twice that of a stock of comparable size with a beta of 1.00.

   F&F go through the same ranking process just discussed but this time keying on beta rather than the ratio of book-to-market value. At mid-year (1963 through 1992), they rank their stocks by beta, smallest in group 1 to largest in group 10.

   They then examine the average values of the book-to-market ratios for each of the ten groups throughout the 1963–90 period.[5]

   The results[6] are shown in Figure 1-3, where we plot book/market against beta.[7]

   They split groups 1 and 10 into two subgroupings, each containing an equal number of stocks. Group 1a has an average beta of 0.5 (very low), and group 10b has an average beta of 1.5 (very high).[8]

   We don't need statistical tests to see the obvious. The high-risk stocks (group 10) are the expensive stocks with the lowest ratios of book-to-market value. The low-risk stocks are the cheap stocks.

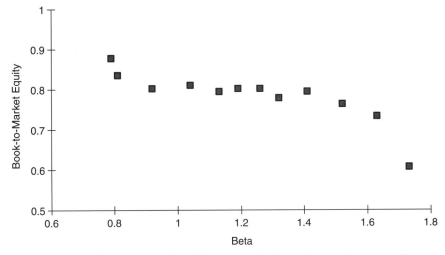

FIGURE 1-3 Book-to-Market of Portfolios Ranked by Beta   *Source*: E. Fama and K. French, "The Cross-Section of Expected Stock Returns," *Journal of Finance*, 1992, pp. 436–437.

The fact that expensive stocks have high risk and low returns and cheap stocks have low risk and high returns brings us to one of the more interesting discoveries of the New Finance.

The riskiest stocks can be expected to produce the lowest future returns and the safest stocks the highest.

In the future, you can expect to get higher returns from public utility stocks than from airline stocks.

Gulp!

Notes

1. E. Fama and K. French, "The Cross-Section of Expected Stock Returns," *The Journal of Finance* (1992).

2. The source of the plot is Table IV from the F&F paper. Break points for the groups are based on yearly decile rankings of NYSE stocks.

3. Kothari, Shanken, and Sloan (S. P. Kothari, J. Shanken, and R. G. Sloan, "Another Look at the Cross-section of Expected Stock Returns," *Journal of Finance* (1995), pp. 185–220) contend that the book/market effect revealed by F&F is due, in part, to the fact that the Compustat tapes (the source of much of F&F's data) contain a survival bias. The tapes were greatly expanded in 1978 to contain data from 6,000 companies. The additional companies were in existence in 1978; however, no companies were added that existed prior to 1978, *but not in 1978*. In another working paper (Harindra de Silva, "What Underlies the Book-to-Market Effect," Graduate School of Management, University of California, Irvine, 1995), the methodology of F&F was replicated on the Compustat tapes over the period 1982 through 1992, a period over which survival bias is not a problem. De Silva finds the following average monthly returns for firms ranked first by size and then by book/market.

Low B/M					High B/M
Big	1.10%	1.19%	1.09%	1.29%	1.48%
	0.50	0.85	0.99	1.23	1.15
	0.20	0.68	0.94	1.13	1.00
	0.61	0.87	0.96	1.16	1.52
Small	2.59	2.98	2.77	3.57	6.91

From this evidence, he concludes that survival bias is not the source of the effect. We will get a better idea of the extent to which the F&F results are influenced by survival bias in Chapter 9, where we estimate the relative *future* expected returns to value stocks and growth stocks. One source of the difference between the record of the past and our expectation for the future might be bias in the record.

4. Short horizons to monitor management performance stem from the fact that the changing nature of techniques and personnel in investment management firms makes longer-term performance generally irrelevant in assessing contemporary skill levels.

5. The groups are formed on the basis of the trailing betas of individual stocks. The betas graphed are computed for the deciles over the period 1963 through 1990.

6. The source of the plot is Table II of the F&F paper.

7. In this case, stocks are ranked annually first by trailing beta (estimated over the past two to five years), which explains the smaller range of book/market ratios.

8. The vast majority of stocks fall in the beta range of 0.40 to 1.60.

CHAPTER 2

The Old Finance

Ironically, the old finance actually goes by the name *Modern Finance.*

But it is rapidly being displaced by radically different ideas, so what was once modern is now becoming old.

In the field of investments, the underpinnings of Modern Finance are contained in three basic concepts:

1. It is possible to build stock portfolios that have the lowest possible risk, given your objective for expected return. Call the technique to build these portfolios *The Tool.*
2. What if we assume *everyone* uses The Tool? Then, when we put together all our portfolios to form a market index like the S&P 500, the S&P, itself, will have the lowest possible risk, given its expected return. This idea, based on the universal use of The Tool, goes by the name Capital Asset Pricing Model (CAPM). We call it *The Theory.*
3. What if, somehow, the prices of *all* stocks always reflected *everything* that was knowable and relevant about them? This notion goes by the name Market Efficiency. Call it *The Fantasy.*

There is nothing wrong with The Tool—other than the fact few investors use it.[1]

This, unfortunately, makes The Theory a sham. If few of us use The Tool to squeeze unnecessary risk from stock portfolios, the market index (if we put *all* of our portfolios of stocks together, we get the market index) won't have the lowest possible risk, given its expected return. Better portfolios can be built with the same expected return and *lower* risk.

One of the claims of The Fantasy is that stock prices react to the revelation of new information very quickly and without bias.

Not true. The evidence stacked against that claim is staggering.

Rather, stock prices *slowly overreact.* Investors tend to overreact to new information about stocks, and they do so with a considerable lag.

As we shall see, this makes it possible to easily build stock portfolios with much *greater* return and much *lower* risk than the S&P 500.

The Tool is cool, but be leery of The Theory.

And fantasies are real only in our dreams.

THE TOOL

Modern Finance was born in 1950 on a spring afternoon on the campus of the University of Chicago.[2] It began in the mind of a young graduate student named Harry Markowitz.

With the aid of J. V. Uspensky's book, *Introduction to Probability,*[3] Harry was working on a problem that would turn out to be part of his Ph.D. dissertation. He was trying to figure out how to build portfolios of stocks with the highest possible expected return given their risk or the lowest possible risk given their expected rate of return.

What is the expected return of a $1 lottery ticket winning the ten-million-dollar jackpot when 20 million tickets have been sold?

Two possible outcomes—(a) $10 million, (b) nothing.

Odds—(a) 1 in 20 million, (b) the rest.

Expected outcome:

$$\$10 \text{ million} \times 1/20 \text{ million} = 50 \text{ cents}$$

Expected return:

$$(50 \text{ cents} - \$1)/\$1.00 = -50\%$$

The odds aren't good, but let's face it—we're paying for the slim hope of becoming wealthy.

Stocks generally have higher expected returns—some as low as 5%; some as high as 25%.

Early into that spring afternoon, Harry discovered that the expected return to a portfolio of stocks is an average of the expected returns to the stocks themselves. Of course, you need to weight the average by the amount you invest in each stock.

Two stocks—one with an expected return of 10%; the other 20%. Invest one-third of your money in the first; two-thirds in the second.

The expected return to the portfolio is:

$$1/3 \times 10\% + 2/3 \times 20\% = 16.67\%$$

That was easy, but by 3:00 P.M., he had accomplished something more difficult. Harry figured out how to calculate the *risk* of a stock portfolio.

Risk: the chances of getting returns different from your expectation.

Also risk: the variability of your return from day to day, from month to month, and from year to year.

AT&T: low risk; United Airlines: high risk.

Harry found that the risk of a portfolio wasn't as easy to calculate as the expected return. Portfolio risk depends not only on the volatility of the stocks within it, but also on how they move relative to each other.

Corn needs lots of rain; artichokes don't. Plant corn on the East 40 and artichokes on the West, and you'll get some kind of crop no matter what.

An increase in the price of oil is good for Exxon but bad for United. Buy both and you won't care if oil goes up or down.

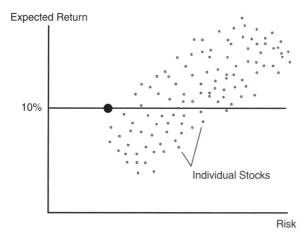

FIGURE 2-1   Lowest-Risk Portfolio with a 10% Return

A low-risk stock portfolio is well diversified. It contains many stocks whose prices are driven by many *different* forces—oil, weather, exchange rates, and so on.

Harry now knew how to compute the risk and expected return to stock portfolios.

But how to find the best portfolios?

By 4:00 P.M. on that spring afternoon, he figured out how to squeeze out the greatest possible amount of risk from a stock portfolio.

Consider Figure 2-1, which plots expected return against risk. The little dots represent the risk and expected return of individual stock investments. Suppose you want a 10% expected return for your portfolio. Some of the individual stocks in Figure 2-1 qualify, but they carry high risk.

Harry figured out how to combine the stocks to drive risk all the way down to the big dot—the lowest-risk combination given an expected return objective (here, 10%). By doing this repeatedly for different return objectives, we can find what MBAs call the *efficient set*, which is depicted in Figure 2-2. These are the portfolios with lowest risk, given expected return and highest expected return, given risk. (From now on, we will call the efficient set "The Bullet.")

Forty years later, Harry would win the Nobel Prize.

Not a bad afternoon's work, I'd say.

THE THEORY

The idea behind The Theory is simple. What would the stock market be like if we *all* used The Tool?[4]

About ten years after the discovery of The Tool, Bill Sharpe (Stanford), John Lintner (Harvard), and Jan Mossin (Bergen) simultaneously, and independently, asked themselves that same question: "What would the market be like if we *all* used The Tool?"[5]

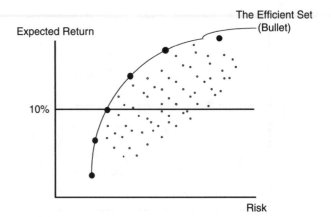

FIGURE 2-2   The Bullet

By 1990, Lintner and Mossin were deceased, so only Sharpe got the Nobel Prize for coming up with The Theory.

The Theory sees us all taking positions on the efficient set, as in Figure 2-3A. The big dots represent the positions of our portfolios. (I haven't drawn them for all of us.)

It's important to understand that for The Theory to work, *all* the big dots must be on the efficient set.[6]

We must *all* use The Tool.[7] (Did you know you were supposed to be using The Tool?)

If we do, then when the dots are added up to form the market index (as in Figure 2-3B), the index itself will be efficient (lowest possible risk given its expected return).

Adding up individual micro-behaviors to get to a collective macro-conclusion.

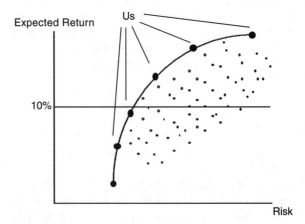

FIGURE 2-3A   Us on the Skin of a Bullet

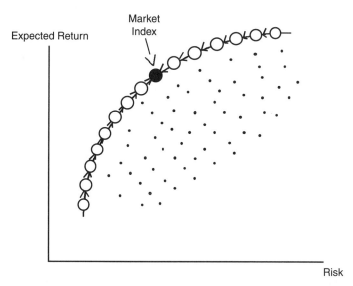

FIGURE 2-3B   We All Make the Market Index

The Theory is like most economic models, where they first assume how individuals will act and then draw conclusions about the *collective effects* of these actions on market prices. As we will discuss in Chapter 12, predictions based on aggregating behaviors can be worthless when individual investors can interact and alter their behaviors accordingly.

In any case, The Theory predicts that the market index is an efficient investment.[8]

If even a *few* of the big dots are beneath the efficient set, the market index will be as well.

Do we all use The Tool?

Don't you remember when you were a teenager? Coming home late from a date. Trying to sneak in through the back door only to find your parents still up. Waiting for *you*? Not a chance. Instead, still struggling to figure out where they should position themselves on The Bullet for the next month.

Don't you remember??

Or the long talks on the phone with your granny? Her words filled with her deep concerns about the peculiar shape of The Bullet this month, and what she should do about it?

Remember???

Okay. So *we* all don't use The Tool, but surely the *pros* must.

Do *they* use The Tool?

Sorry, Harry. You'd have to look for a long, long time before you'd find a single money manager using The Tool to help manage the *volatility* of his or her stock portfolio.[9]

You see, *stock managers don't care much about the volatility of their return.*[10]

They *do* watch their "bets" in industries and sectors. They *are* careful about how much they invest in any one stock.

And many *do* care very much about *tracking error* relative to their benchmark portfolios (like the S&P 500).

Tracking error?

Tracking error—the volatility of the *differences* between the returns to their portfolio and the returns to their benchmark.

Minimize tracking error and you minimize the probability of underperforming by an amount sufficient to get you fired by the pension fund that hired you.

Those managers who manage risk in a quantitative way do it with a version of The Tool that manages *tracking error*—not volatility of return.

But The Theory's efficient set is dimensioned in terms of *volatility*—not *tracking error.*

So you see, the pros aren't trying for The Theory's efficient set either.

Almost *none* of them are.[11]

But The Theory assumes they *all* are.

Us included.

And in spite of the rather obvious fact that very few of us actually attempt to hold portfolios positioned on The Bullet, one of the favorite pastimes of finance professors is to run complicated tests to see if the prediction of The Theory is true.

Is the market index on the efficient set?

Based on the results revealed in this book and casual observation of professional and nonprofessional investor behavior, I can confidently say, "No."

Some professors have even gone so far as to see if the prediction was true in periods *prior* to the invention of The Tool.

How could we all have been out there using The Tool in 1950, and earlier, when it wasn't invented yet?

Did Napoleon drive a Ferrari to Waterloo?

These professors *must* be joking.[12]

THE FANTASY

There are still some finance professors who fantasize about a stock market dominated by an army of professional, rational, and driven investors who search in every nook and cranny for clues that might lead them to the discovery of an undervalued stock.

When they find a clue, they act—quickly. Their trades push stock prices, which quickly adjust to reflect the information in the clues.

Never mind about the trades of the "little guys" who don't have a clue about Modern Finance.

Never mind that *we* are driven by greed and fear.

Our emotions allegedly have no impact on stock prices, because "the professional army" is very effective at policing the level of prices in the market.

Many professors hold on to The Fantasy with the tenacity of religious zealots.

Take a Zealot to the top of the Himalayas. Point to the fossilized shell of a sea animal, and ask him how it got there if the world is only a few thousand years old.

Zealot: "Simple. God put it there to confuse heretics like you."

Heretic: "Sir, while I must admit that's a possibility, I believe there's a more plausible explanation."

Many Heretics are now finding "fossils" in financial data that should convince all but the most ardent of the Zealots.

Notes

1. Except at asset allocation levels where institutions such as pension funds use it to determine how much of their funds should be invested in asset *classes* like bonds and stock. The Tool is also used by quantitative investment managers to manage the volatility of the *differences* between the returns on their long and short portfolios. Hedge funds actually build portfolios of stocks that they sell short. In effect, long-only managers are "short" their benchmarks like the S&P 500 stock index.

2. True story.

3. J. V. Upensky, *Introduction to Mathematical Probability* (New York: McGraw-Hill Book Company, 1937).

4. Actually, The Theory assumes that we all use The Tool *without restriction.* Thus, if you were to sell a stock short, The Theory assumes you can do anything you want with the proceeds. In the real world, you would probably be required by those who lend you the stocks you short to invest the proceeds of selling short in cash. If *any* of us were restricted in this way, The Theory wouldn't hold even if we *all* used The Tool.

5. J. Lintner, "The Valuation of Risk Assets and the Selection of Risky Investments on Stock Portfolios and Capital Budgets," *Review of Economics and Statistics* (February 1965); J. Mossin, "Equilibrium in a Capital Market," *Econometrica* (October 1966); and W. F. Sharpe, "Capital Asset Prices: A Theory of Market Equilibrium," *Journal of Finance* (September 1964).

6. Modern Finance (like Behavioral Finance) works from an assumed structure for individual decision making to the asset pricing implications of this structure. For example, a Modern Finance person might assume that, for all investors, utility or well-being increases as a quadratic function of the investor's wealth. Under this assumption, the investor can make choices between alternative investments in terms of their expected return and the volatility of the return. Rational investors will then assume positions on The Tool's efficient set based on the exact nature of their utility functions. The asset pricing implication of these assumptions is a linear relationship between expected return and beta. A behavioral finance person may amend the utility function to account for certain less than rational behaviors. These behaviors will also carry their own asset pricing implications. In both cases, we go from (micro) assumed decision-making frameworks for individuals to (macro) pricing implications. In both cases, we employ a *deductive* methodology. The New Finance differentiates itself in that it employs *inductive* methodologies to investigate the asset pricing structure itself. As you will see in Chapter 12, the deductive process stemming from the decision-making by individuals fails to account for the complexity arising from the myriad of unique interactions of individual decision makers.

7. In the context of The Tool, The Theory predicts that the cap-weighted market portfolio be on what Markowitz called the *critical line* (the line showing the weights for the portfolios on the bullet). *Other than by sher chance, the only way we can expect that this will be true is if all investors hold portfolios that are also positioned somewhere on the critical line.* This being the case, when we aggregate, we get the predicted efficiency of the cap-weighted market portfolio. Advocates of CAPM can't lean on the notion that its predictions will be enforced by rational traders buying and selling at the margin. These traders have no incentive to trade so as to make the aggregate market index mean–variance efficient. Suppose all investors hold mean–variance efficient portfolios except for your grandmother, who for reasons of her own, chooses to hold a one-stock portfolio (AT&T). Rational traders still have an incentive to assume

positions on the critical line. Your grandmother's holdings of AT&T (off the line) are nevertheless aggregated, along with the others, to form the market portfolio. Rational traders have no incentive to prevent your grandmother from spoiling CAPM's central prediction.

8. The Theory thus provides a convenient intellectual rationale for institutional investors, such as pension funds for indexing or building equity composites (the combined portfolios of their equity managers) that look like the aggregate market index. Although many pension officers actually believe in The Theory, and even in The Fantasy, most invest passively or collectively in the market index because this investment reduces their fear of embarrassment from underperforming the index.

9. Some of the more quantitative managers do use what are called risk factor models to help them manage the potential for their portfolios to deviate from their benchmarks (usually the S&P 500). But these managers aren't attempting to minimize portfolio risk as The Theory defines it.

10. Volatility is the standard deviation of a series of returns.

11. Andrew Rudd, former CEO of Barra, the world's largest vendor of professional investment software, has told me that not a single client of theirs uses their tool to manage volatility of return. They all use it to manage tracking error.

12. In L. Chan and J. Lakonishok, "Are Reports of Beta's Death Premature?" *Journal of Portfolio Management* the authors state, in relation to the CAPM, "If anything, then, the model seems to work too well until the mid-fifties. It is possible that Markowitz's ideas were not so new after all, and the marginal investor knew how to form efficient portfolios long before Markowitz was born." As discussed in Note 7 above, marginal investors cannot enforce the predictions of The Theory. Moreover, we should point out that the authors fail to control for size in their regressions. As we shall see in Chapter 6, this is crucial in a test of the relationship between risk and expected return.

13. See R. Haugen and N. Baker, "Case Closed," which provides irrefutable evidence that the stock market is highly inefficient. It can be downloaded free of charge at http://ssrn.com/abstract=1306523.

CHAPTER 3

How Long Is the Short Run?

THE SHORT RUN AND THE LONG RUN

Remember something you learned in Economics 101?

Normal profit: what is fair and reasonable given the size of the capital investment, the prevailing level of interest rates, and the risk associated with the firm's line of business.

Abnormal profit: when a firm earns more or less than that.

In Economics 101, our professors told us that firms in competitive lines of business can earn abnormal profits only in the *short run.* In the *long run*, firms can, among other things, invest (or disinvest) additional capital into lines of business, and additional competitors may come to bear. Competitors enter profitable lines of business, driving prices down and taking away market share—driving profits down to normal levels. Competitors leave unprofitable lines, allowing companies that remain to increase revenues, perhaps raise prices and make the most of a higher market share—driving profits up to normal levels. Companies that leave those lines reinvent themselves elsewhere—reverting to average or normal profit levels in this way.

But our Economics 101 professors forgot to tell us something that turns out to be very important.

Just how long *is* the short run, anyway?

We know that the length of the short run varies over different lines of business. The barriers to entry in some lines are much more formidable than in others. The short run for Coca-Cola, for example, will probably extend over a long, long time. People like the taste of Coke, and the formula is a secret.

But surely there is an *average* expected length of the short run over all lines of business. Just how long is it on average?

A major theme in this book is that the short run typically lasts for only a few years at most.

Prices in the inefficient market, however, do not reflect this. They tend to mistakenly project a continuation of abnormal profit levels for long periods into the future. Because of this, successful firms become overvalued. Unsuccessful firms become undervalued. Then, as the process of competitive entry and exit drives performance to the mean faster than expected, investors in the formerly expensive stocks become disappointed with reported earnings, and investors in the formerly cheap stocks are pleasantly surprised.

In this book we present *very convincing evidence* that this is indeed the case.

For starters, consider a study by two UCLA professors, Jegadeesh and Titman (JT).[1] Their study provides important insight about how the market reacts to announcements of success or lack thereof by business firms.

First, JT classify stocks as winners or losers, and then they measure their *subsequent* relative performance.[2] Winners are defined as the 10% of stocks in their sample that had the best returns over the *past* six months, and losers are defined as the 10% with the worst returns.

They then observe the relative performance of the winners and losers over three-day periods within each of the next 36 months. Each month, they measure the performance of firms reporting earnings in that month. They measure returns for those firms only during the two days preceding and on the day of the announcement of quarterly earnings per share.

To illustrate, in the *first month* following the ranking of the winners and losers, JT would focus only on those companies that reported earnings *in that month*. For these firms, they look at the difference between the returns for winners and losers *only in the three-day vicinity of the earnings announcement dates (the two days before and the day of)*.

As we see in Figure 3-1A, in which we are plotting the monthly differences in the returns between the winners and losers, the winners of the past do better in the first month following "now"[3] and also in the seven months that follow.[4]

Apparently, the market is being pleasantly surprised by the earnings reports of the winners during the first seven months and unpleasantly surprised by the losers.[5]

The winners probably reported good earnings in the trailing six-month period. The losers likely reported bad earnings. We speak of good and bad relative to market expectations, so these respective earnings are "surprises."

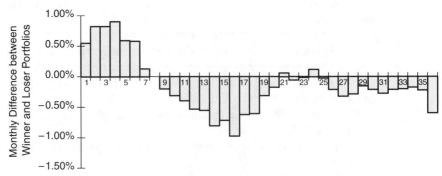

FIGURE 3-1A   Monthly Difference Between Winner and Loser Portfolios at Announcement Dates   *Source*: N. Jegadeesh and S. Titman, "Returns to Buying Winners and Selling Losers: Implications for Market Efficiency," *Journal of Finance* (1993), p. 88.

The market's reaction in the seven months that follow the trailing six reflects its failure to recognize that good quarterly reports foretell of a *few* more good ones to follow; and that bad quarterly reports foretell of a few bad ones coming. The subsequent good or bad reports catch the market by surprise, and the winners outperform the losers as they are reported.

A rational, efficient market would be aware of this tendency. It would anticipate the following good and bad reports in advance and wouldn't have to react upon their arrival.[6]

But look what happens after the eighth month.

Now, the stocks previously classified as *losers* are showing superior returns at the earnings announcement dates.[7] Note that this tendency holds *consistently*, month after month.

Apparently, the market overreacted to its surprises of the eight months before and the six months before that.

The market became convinced that the string of good (or bad) reports over the past 14 months were precursors of *many* more to follow.

They *were* not.

After the eighth month, the market is being pleasantly surprised at the unexpectedly good reports of the past losers and is unpleasantly surprised by the past winners.

This is your first look at evidence pointing to the conclusion that firms quickly *revert to the mean* in terms of the growth rates they report in earnings per share.

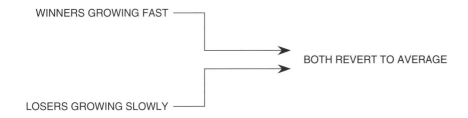

The good, as well as the bad, quickly become the average.

Mean reversion that takes place more quickly than expected.

Presumably, the unsuccessful, cheap value stocks are leaving behind their negative abnormal profits, and the successful, expensive growth stocks are leaving behind their positive abnormal profits.

This pattern is apparent in Figure 3-1B, which shows the cumulative difference in the returns of the winners and losers. By the time we get to the 36th month, the losers have outperformed the winners on a cumulative basis.[8] This implies that the sum of the initial six-month performance and the performance in the subsequent eight-month period was an overreaction that has finally been corrected.

The market overreacts—but with a lag.

The clumsy, inefficient market can't even make its *mistakes* quickly.

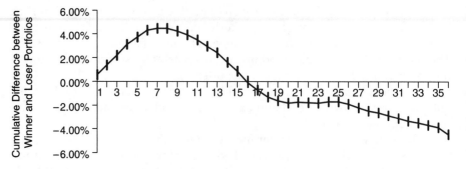

FIGURE 3-1B   Cumulative Difference Between Winner and Loser Portfolios at Announcement Dates

THE ENGINE THAT DRIVES US TO DIAMOND HEAD

The pattern revealed in Figures 3-1A and 3-1B is a recurring one that appears in the results of other studies. In the six-month period during which the winners and losers were named, the winners obviously outperformed. But they *continue* their winning ways in the next seven months that follow.

In the intermediate term,[9] stocks that do well have a tendency to continue to do so. Stocks that do badly sink even further for a while.

The market failed to recognize that good earnings reports have a tendency to signal more to follow *just around the corner.* Failing to recognize this, positive price reactions to the initial news tend to be followed by more positive reactions to the news that follows.

And the converse tends to be true for the bad-news stocks:

$$+ \text{ followed by } +$$
$$- \text{ followed by } -$$

Inertia in the intermediate term.[10]

But the sums of the $+\ +$ and the $-\ -$ tend to be *overreactions.* And these overreactions tend to be corrected after the inertia dissipates.

The market overreacts because it believes that a *sequence* of positive or negative announcements foretells of an *extended* series of future announcements of the same sign.

The market believes that growth stocks will continue to grow and value stocks will continue to languish.

This is a mistake, and when the market sees the extended series coming out mixed rather than consistent, it corrects the price, *reversing* the initial inertia pattern.

As we see in Figures 3-1A and 3-1B, the correction takes place over an extended period, but its magnitude is rather dramatic, and it truly is the *engine* that drives GO.

+ + followed by −

− − followed by +

Inertia in the *intermediate term*[11] followed by *reversals* in the *long term*.

We will get to Diamond Head by investing in cheap value stocks. Today's cheap stocks have experienced the − − *in the past.* By buying them at cheap prices today, we get the + *in the future.*

Interestingly, we can confirm these patterns in stock prices by looking at *volatility* of return, where return is measured over different intervals—weeks, months, years, and numbers of years.

Volatility is a measure of the extent to which a stock's returns can differ from month to month or from year to year.

Consider Figure 3-2. We plot two periods of time along the horizontal axis. (We'll define the length of the periods later.) Stock price is plotted vertically.

The solid lines are consistent with inertia in stock prices—increases follow increases; declines follow declines. The broken lines are consistent with reversals.

Suppose we measure returns over one-period intervals (from 0 to 1). The range of possible return is the same regardless of whether we're dealing with inertia or reversal patterns.

But if return is, instead, measured over a two-period interval (from 0 to 2), the range is much greater if inertia is present than if we're dealing with reversals.

If returns have inertia patterns, increase the length of the return interval and volatility should go up rather quickly.

If returns tend to reverse direction, increase the length of the return interval and volatility should go up more slowly and perhaps even fall.[12]

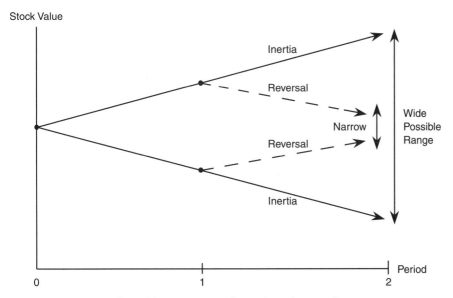

FIGURE 3-2   Range of Possible Outcomes with Inertia and Reversal Patterns

Suppose the length of the interval plotted on the horizontal axis of Figure 3-2 is in weeks. If *inertia* is present in stock prices in the short run (over a few months), we should see volatility go up quickly as the number of weeks used to calculate the return is increased. With inertia, as we increase the return interval, we dramatically increase the range of possibilities for the return. If returns persist in direction from week to week, the return for the next month can be very large or very small, depending on whether the month begins with an advance or a decline. Advances feed further advances. Declines feed declines.

If, instead, weekly returns tend to reverse, initial advances or declines will tend to be erased by subsequent movements in the opposite direction, keeping the *monthly* return from becoming extremely large or extremely small (negative).

Let's see what happens to volatility of return when we increase the return interval from weeks to months.

Figure 3-3 plots the results of a study by two professors from MIT and the University of Pennsylvania, Andrew Lo and Craig MacKinlay (LM).[13] LM form stocks into three portfolios containing small, medium, and large companies.[14]

The vertical axis plots the level of volatility *as a percentage of what it should be if there were no inertia or reversal patterns present.*[15] The horizontal axis plots the number of weeks used in measuring the return. Note that as the number of weeks used in calculating the return increases, the volatility becomes increasingly excessive, relative to what it should be in the noninertia (or nonreversal) case.[16] This pattern becomes more pronounced as the size of the companies becomes smaller. Thus, the smaller stocks are characterized by more inertia than the larger stocks.

Inertia in the intermediate term.

The market does not catch on to the fact that a positive event is a precursor of a *few* more positive events to follow. A good earnings report, for example,

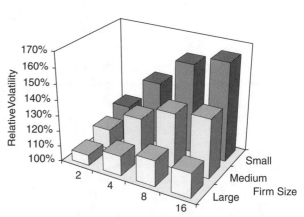

FIGURE 3-3 Volatility Relative to a Series with No Reversals or Inertia   *Source*: A. W. Lo and A. C. MacKinlay, "Stock Prices Do Not Follow Random Walks: Evidence from a Simple Specification Test," *Review of Financial Studies* (1988), Table 2.

usually foretells of a few more to follow. Failing to recognize this, the market's reaction to the first report is incomplete. A complete reaction of an *efficient* market would reflect revised expectations for *more* good earnings reports in the next few quarters. There would be no need for further positive reactions in the next few quarters as the good reports come in as expected.

On the other hand, there is evidence of *reversal patterns* in stock prices when returns are measured over much *longer periods of time*.

Suppose the length of the interval plotted in Figure 3-2 is much longer, say, in *years*. If *reversal* patterns are present over periods of a few *years* rather than weeks, we should see volatility go up more slowly as the number of years used to calculate the return is increased. Strong moves up or down in the initial part of the return period will tend to be erased by reversing moves later on in the period, keeping the return over the total period in a narrow range. (This keeps volatility of return down.)

Let's see if volatility actually grows much more slowly as the return interval is increased to periods of years rather than weeks.

Figure 3-4 plots the results of a study by Poterba and Summers (PS).[17] Summers was the former Secretary of the Treasury under Bill Clinton. The basic nature of the graph is identical to Figure 3-3, but this time, we are dealing with years instead of weeks, and we are dealing with different countries rather than with groups of different sizes.[18] Note that in every country the volatility is less than you would expect it to be in the absence of reversal patterns.

REVERSALS IN THE LONG TERM. Once the *run* of a few positive or negative events materializes, the market develops a belief that the run will persist for *long periods* into the future. For example, if a firm's earnings per share has

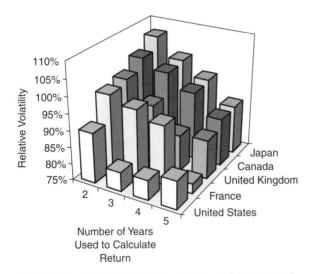

FIGURE 3-4   Volatility Relative to a Series with No Reversals or Inertia   *Source*: J. Poterba and L. Summers, "The Persistence of Volatility and Stock Returns: Evidence and Implications," *Journal of Financial Economics* (1988), Table 4.

grown fast for the last three quarters, the market believes that this foretells of continued success for *many more* quarters into the future. The price of the stock becomes inflated on the basis of this expectation. But the market is wrong. Past success does not foretell of *prolonged* success in the future. As this becomes apparent *much later*, the past inflation in the market price of the stock begins to reverse, creating a long-term reversal pattern in the returns.

Considering the results of LM and PS together, we have confirmation of a market that is *slow* to *overreact*.

I wonder how the Zealots justify their continued belief in The Fantasy in view of these "fossils"?

Notes

1. N. Jegadeesh and S. Titman, "Returns to Buying Winners and Selling Losers: Implications for Stock Market Efficiency," *Journal of Finance* (1993).

2. The JT study covers the period 1980 through 1989. Thus, it avoids the survival bias problem in the Compustat tapes. The study includes all firms on the New York and American stock exchanges for which the required data were available.

3. There are actually a series of "nows," one for each year of their study. The results are then averaged over all the "nows."

4. These results can be confirmed by some earlier results in the accounting literature. See, for example, V. Bernard and J. K. Thomas, "Post-Earning-Announcement Drift: Delayed Price Response or Risk Premium," *Journal of Accounting Research* (Supplement 1989); V. Bernard and J. K. Thomas, "Evidence That Stock Prices Do Not Fully Reflect the Implications of Current Earnings for Future Earnings," *Journal of Accounting and Economics* (1990); and J. B. Wiggins, "Do Misconceptions about the Earnings Process Contribute to Post-Announcement Drift?" unpublished manuscript (Ithaca, NY: Cornell University).

5. The monthly difference in "announcement day" performance is statistically significant at least at the 5% level for months 1 through 7.

6. As we will later see for long-term corrections of overreactions, N. Jegadeeesh and S. Titman, "Profitability of Momentum Strategies: An Evaluation of Alternative Explanations," *Journal of Finance* (April 2001), find an interesting seasonal pattern in intermediate-term momentum. They find that winners outperform in all months save January. In January, the losers outperform.

7. The monthly difference in the performance of the winners and losers is significant at the 5% level in months 11 through 18, and the losers outperform the winners in every month except 21 and 24.

8. To obtain the returns implied by Figure 3-1B, you would have to trade in the portfolio so as to be invested at the beginning of each month in the stocks that are expected to report earnings for the month.

9. There are also *short-term reversal* patterns in stock returns. If a stock did relatively well in the past one or two months, it will have a tendency to do poorly in the next month. These reversal patterns may be caused by investor overreaction to various events and the resulting price pressure—someone trying to buy or sell a lot of the stock forcing its price above or below its equilibrium value—a move that's corrected later.

10. As distinguished from the short or long run discussed earlier.

11. In M. Lee and B. Swaminathan, "Price Momentum and Trading Volume," *Journal of Finance* (October 2000), evidence is presented that the momentum effect is roughly three times as great for stocks with high volume in the previous six months than for stocks with low volume.

12. If we square the volatility, we get the variance. If there are no reversal or inertia patterns present in the series (if the series is random), then the variance can be expected to be proportional to the length of the return interval. The variance of annual returns should be 12 times the variance of monthly returns.

13. A. W. Lo and A. C. MacKinlay, "Stock Market Prices Do Not Follow Random Walks: Evidence from a Simple Specification Test," *The Review of Financial Studies* (Spring 1988).

14. Their study covers a number of stocks ranging from 2036 to 2720, depending on the point in time. All stocks are from the New York and American stock exchanges. The time period for their analysis extended from September 1962 through December 1985. Returns include both dividends as well as capital gains.

15. That is, if the series were random and variance is proportional to the length of the return interval.

16. All of the volatility ratios are significantly greater than 100% with greater than 95% confidence.

17. J. Poterba and L. Summers, "Mean Reversion in Stock Prices," *Journal of Financial Economics* (December 1988).

18. For all countries except Canada and the United Kingdom, the time period covered was 1957 to 1986. For Canada, the period was 1919 to 1986, and for the United Kingdom, it was 1939 to 1986. All returns are adjusted for inflation and do not include dividends. Poterba and Summers test for the effects of excluding dividends in the returns by replicating the test with dividends on the U.S. and UK markets. These results show only minor differences resulting from dividend omission.

CHAPTER 4

The Ancient Finance

GROWTH STOCKS WEREN'T ALWAYS

To continue this story, we need to move to a different place in time and space.[1]

September 24, 1925.

Manhattan Island. Midtown. A curb on 43rd Street. Flooded from the morning's rain. Now approached by a speeding car, the right front wheel of which is about to displace a significant fraction of said flood and send it hurtling toward a rather distinguished gentleman standing on the sidewalk.

<pre>
                        E
                        d
                        g
              t.   a
                        r
        a
                        L
     l   a
   p   w
  S   Lawrence Smith knew this wasn't to be his day.
</pre>

The '23 Pierce-Arrow sped through the rest of the puddle and down the street without even as much as an afterthought.

Edgar now had the appearance of someone who had recently emerged from a morning's wade through the Atlantic.

He beat his umbrella furiously at the coupe as it rounded the corner down Fifth Avenue. **IMBECILE!!!**

His fury wasn't due to the ruination of his trousers as much as it was to the need of dry trousers to properly address the Harvard Economic Society.

In five minutes!

Completing his walk to the Harvard Club, he entered the building, walked through the reading room, which reeked of many generations of securely settled tobacco smoke, and entered the meeting room where he was to give his address.

The room was filled with 50 or so members of the society dressed in *perfectly dry* business attire. He was immediately greeted by Jonathan Crestview, president of the society and the man who had arranged for Edgar to speak.

"Mr. Smith, thank you so much for coming to enlighten us today. We're all very much looking forward to hearing about your book. But what happened to you? You look like you just took a dip in the Atlantic. Shall I get you a towel?"

"I'll be okay. Sometimes I think we were better off with horses and buggies. Horses are more civil than New Yorkers, even on their best days."

To hide his condition from the rest, Edgar stood behind the podium and let Crestview introduce him from the side.

"GENTLEMEN! Gentlemen! Please be seated. We have the good fortune to have with us today Mr. Edgar Lawrence Smith, author of the much discussed book, *Common Stocks as Long-Term Investments*.[2] As you know, the book contains some findings and views that most of us feel are very, well, controversial. We now have the opportunity to engage in an interchange that should help to enlighten us all on these matters. Mr. Smith, perhaps you would like to begin."

Edgar spread his notes before him, and began with the tabulations that filled most of the book. Edgar had spent the last several years painstakingly documenting the performance of the common stocks and bonds issued by some of the largest U.S. corporations. He began with the year 1836 and tracked the performance of the two types of securities in various periods through 1923.

His finding: In terms of their annual rate of return, common stocks had outstripped bonds by a wide margin over this extended period of time. This happened not only over the extended period, but also over most subperiods as well.

First confrontation. From the back of the room.

"But Mr. Smith, surely, the wide gap in the returns between stocks and bonds was due to the unfolding of the particular events of the last 60 years. Had times been less favorable, the gap would have been much more narrow, perhaps even nonexistent."

"I don't doubt that, but notice that the gap reappears in all the periods in which return is measured."

"Are you seriously asking us to believe that such a gap can be expected to persist over the *next* 60 years? That's, quite simply, preposterous!"

"I don't believe I've asked you to believe anything of the sort. My numbers simply document what has happened in the past. You can judge for yourself what lies ahead in the future."

Now Edgar moved into what he knew was to be the most controversial part of his talk—valuing common stocks based on their potential *future* prospects.

"Let me now review the fundamental process that leads us to our estimates of the intrinsic value of common shares. As you well know, we must place principle effort in standardizing the numbers reported on income statements and balance sheets to reconcile the widely divergent standards applied by accountants in measuring the income and wealth of firms. I do not wish to argue here today over the means by which these numbers are standardized, for I regard these means as fitting and proper. It is not the standardization itself that will be the focus of my comments. Rather, it will be the *objective* of the analysis that will be my focus.

"The fundamental underpinning of our analysis is, and always has been, the *current*, normalized value of earnings per share. It is also true that most of us modify this value to reflect any abnormalities we perceive in the current state of business conditions. We grope for an estimate of the earning power of the firm in a state of 'normal' business conditions."

"This number, normalized, *current* earnings becomes the basis of our estimates of stock intrinsic value. To be sure, the multiples we apply to this number are somewhat different for different stocks, but the differences are currently based on our perceptions of the quality of the earnings or the relative risk of the companies."

"I am before you today to state that there is another, much neglected factor in the intrinsic value calculation."

An initial buzz of excitement in the room. Then, quiet anticipation.

A small puddle had formed at Edgar's feet.

"My results clearly show that a well-diversified investment in common stocks may be counted on for a definite increase in principal value. But not all stocks have the same potential for this increase in principal. In estimating the intrinsic value for a stock, it is my feeling that we can quite properly consider the potential for principal enhancement *in the future*."

More noise from the crowd now. Much more. You might even call it a roar of sorts.

From the middle of the room a rather stout analyst named Bekker stood up. "Growth? Do you mean future growth in normalized earnings?"

"Why, yes. Enhancement in principal would be related to that."

Bekker: "That's heresy! We *all* agree here that future growth is a *speculative* and not an *investment* consideration!"

Edgar knew what Bekker meant. Investment considerations were things that you could predict and count on to some degree. Speculative considerations were basically the result of chance. Unpredictable.

Smith: "My results indicate that there *has been* a wide range of principal enhancement associated with different common stocks. It seems only reasonable that different stocks have different potentials for principal enhancement *in the future*. Those with the greatest potential should also command the greatest multiples."

From the front of the room: "And what evidence are you prepared to show us to support this contention?"

"The high returns on stocks relative to bonds result from the fact that the stock prices of the past did not reflect the potential for appreciation that was, in fact, to come. If the analysts of the past had taken this potential for future growth into account, stock returns would have been more reasonable in relation to bond returns. I'm simply asking us now to correct the mistakes that were made in the past."

After many more exchanges, Edgar, the heretic, actually thought he might be making some progress. But then he ran out of time.

Saying goodbye to Crestview, Edgar said, "Thank you for the invitation to speak about my book. Tell me, what do you now think about my views?"

"To tell you the truth, Mr. Smith, I feel now as I felt when we first met today."

"Really. And how is that?"

"I do believe you're all wet!"

THE NEW ERA

By 1929 Smith's *Common Stocks as Long-Term Investments* had become a best-seller.

Expected future growth, as the underpinning of stock value, had become the established point of view. A reasonable price, in relation to current normalized earnings, was no longer required for the prudent investor. Future growth had now become an *investment* as opposed to a *speculative* consideration.

To see the change in standards, consider the following interchange from the "Answers to Inquiries" section of the *Wall Street Journal* from February 26, 1924:

> Question: Would you suggest some railroad stock to purchase? The idea is to buy something likely to appreciate in price, as well as to continue paying income.
>
> Answer: We cannot advise you as to stocks that are likely to appreciate in value, since it is contrary to our policy to give speculative advice. The following are stocks that hold places of prominence as established earners and dividend payers in the railroad group: New York Central, Atchison, Southern Pacific, Chesapeake and Ohio, Union Pacific, Illinois Central, Baltimore & Ohio and Atlantic Coast line.

Now consider a front-page article on the motor industry in the *Journal* on January 7, 1929:

> Practically without exception leaders in the industry predict new high records in motor output for the year and continued prosperity for motor manufacturers. When one looks at the (market) values that are being offered at this time, it hardly seems believable, yet I will venture to predict that with the spirit of progress that has prevailed from the beginning and still prevails in the industry, the end has in no sense been reached.

Or the following from the *Journal's* "Inquiring Investor" column on the outlook for Northwest Engineering, written on February 21, 1929:

> . . . on the basis of the company's estimated earnings and outlook, the stock could hardly be said to be overpriced, and the matter of (dividend) yield would probably be adjusted through an upward

revision in the dividend rate paid if present estimates of future earnings materialize.

As the general level of prices advanced upward in 1929, the spreads in price-to-earnings multiples began to widen dramatically. The *Wall Street Journal*, March 2, 1929:

> It is evident that more attention is being given to values than hereto-fore. This explains the fact that many stocks have been moving ahead more rapidly than others. The issues representing industries that have been making substantial progress have been most favored. It is likely this tendency will continue.

Expected future growth became the modern concept. Investing based on established performance was now old-fashioned. Consider Charles Schwab's comments in the *Journal* on March 8, 1929:

> Mr. Schwab says he no longer sees danger in the situation. "Last year my conclusions were based on old fashioned ideas," says Mr. Schwab. "Everyone has made money except the old timers."
> Mr. Schwab merely repeats the views of many other old timers. As one remarked: "I have made nothing in the market for the reason that I got my Wall Street education 20 years too soon. The younger minds are not troubled with past performance. They do not remember the numerous panics and periods of stress as we old timers do. They are looking into the future. We are looking into the past. They have plenty of imagination. Our imagination is warped by events of the past. We made a mistake and will have to admit it, as Mr. Schwab has done."

This focus on the future by a new generation of investors is revealed in the "Broad Street Gossip" column in the edition of the *Journal* published on June 15, 1929:

> It's not so much what a company is earning now as what average earnings will be in years to come.

This fundamental change in investment standards evolved as the entire country looked to the future with increasing confidence. Herbert Hoover spoke of the "New Era" in which cooperation in business, aided by government and guided by scientific principles, would lead to prosperity for the nation and greater freedom in all aspects of life.

The new, modern investment philosophy came to be known as the "New Era Theory."

In *The Great Bull Market*,[3] Robert Sobel writes of it:

> In the past they said stock prices reflected the present because the future was uncertain. Now, however the nation was enjoying

permanent prosperity; depressions were no longer possible. If you *knew* that a company's earnings were increasing at a rate of 20 per cent a year, it was clear that they would double in less than five years if compounded. Would it not be wise to take these anticipated earnings into consideration? In the past stocks sold at ten times earnings. The stock which sold at fifteen times earnings in 1928 was, in reality, selling at less than eight times 1933 earnings and so was more conservative a purchase than it would have been a decade earlier.

Before the first traces of the scent of the impending economic storm were to blow across the shores of Manhattan Island, the *Wall Street Journal* wrote on August 7, 1929:

Now we have come into the jazz age, and principles which have not been established by facts are ignored, they are subordinated in new experiences and more fruitful maxims. We may say that the deductive method of accepting certain stereotyped premises and investing strictly in accord with them has been abandoned for the inductive method of accumulating our own facts and establishing our own principles. This change has brought common stocks into high favor with special emphasis on companies which have possibilities of continuous expansion over an indefinite period.

But as the "modern" investors of the late 1920s were soon to learn, depressions were far from impossible. The New Era Theory was about to collapse under the weight of the great stock market crash of October 1929, which served as the gateway to the Great Depression of the 1930s.

Later, in the midst of the rubble of the financial and economic debacle, two men, Graham and Dodd, who were to wield great influence in the decades to come, wrote the first edition of their book *Security Analysis*. In this book, they attacked the tenets of the New Era Theory. Graham and Dodd felt that future growth was largely, if not completely, unpredictable. They were particularly opposed to estimating future earnings by extrapolating from past trend:

Value based on a satisfactory trend must be wholly arbitrary and hence speculative, and hence inevitably subject to exaggeration and later collapse.[4]

Their book was to become the bible of the investment business. It evolved through several editions, but Graham and Dodd held steadfast to their views. In the 1951 edition, they write:

The analyst's philosophy must still compel him to base his investment valuation on an assumed earning power no larger than the company has already achieved in some year of normal business. Investment value can be related only to demonstrated performance.[5]

Graham and Dodd maintained their influence throughout most of the 1950s. But as the great bull market of the 1950s commenced and marched onward and upward, a "new" philosophy began to emerge. Once again, the likes of Graham and Dodd cried heresy!

But the new philosophy once again took hold—stock prices should properly be based on future prospects for growth.

Only those who put their ears to the rail and listened *very* carefully were able to discern that these *new* thoughts were merely *echoes* of the sounds made by Growth Train #1, which had rumbled its way through New York Station some 30 years before.

By 1960, growth stock investing was *back*.

As with its emergence in the 1920s, its arrival was not heralded by published evidence documenting that either (a) the "old timers" (many of whom were now the *children* of the young hot shots of the 1920s) were wrong about future growth not being subject to reliable forecasts or (b) the nature of the world had now changed and the relative growth rates of two companies could now be reliably projected for extended periods of time into the future.

No evidence whatsoever that either (a) or (b) was true was ever put on the table.

Some old, old timers did experience some *déjà vu*, however.

Just as E. L. Smith's book preceded Train #1 in 1925, in 1954, businessman Winthrop Walker published, *A Re-examination of Common Stocks as Long-Term Investments.*[6] In it, he extended Edgar's study to cover the period 1923–51. Walker concludes:

> Our prudent investor can justifiably conclude . . . that he can continue to hold his common stocks with the confident prospect that over the long-term he will enjoy not only greater income return than from bonds, but also a greater protection for his capital.

These results were to be buttressed ten years later when two professors from the University of Chicago published the results of a study of the performance of common stocks traded on the New York Stock Exchange during the period from 1926 through 1959.[7] They found that, on average, the stocks had earned approximately 9% per annum—an extraordinarily high number, given the relatively low yields to be had on bonds at that time.

Although Growth Train #1 was launched by Smith's single book, which (a) documented the relatively strong performance of common stocks in the past and (b) suggested that current stock values should properly be based on future prospects, Growth Train #2 was supported by the accompaniment of several publications in which ideas (a) and (b) were offered separately.

MIT professor Myron Gordon suggested (b).

In his book, published in 1962, Gordon writes:

> In our stock price model a future dividend expectation is what an investor buys. However, *he is not considered so naive as to assume that*

every future dividend is equal to the current dividend. He is interested in both the current dividend and its rate of growth.[8]

Gordon goes on to set forth complicated mathematical models designed to capture the determinants of the value of common stock. And the centerpiece of these models was the *future rate of growth of earnings and dividends per share.*

None of the publications attempt to *debunk* the old timers' contentions that future growth is speculative and not subject to reliable forecasts. Instead, it seems that both Growth Trains came through riding the crests of bull markets.

Bull markets in which current prices could no longer be justified on the basis of standards that had been applied in the past.

The general level of prices could only be justified as compared to the expected *future* level of earnings.

And if you were going to justify the *general level* of prices on this basis, why not justify the *relative structure* of prices in the same way. Growth stocks command premium *prices* because they have premium *prospects.*

As a happy rider on Growth Train #2 in 1968, Robert Sobel concluded that:

> . . . price/earnings were unreasonable in 1928–1929 only when compared with those of 1920 and earlier; when placed side by side with those of today they appear sensible and even a bit on the low side.
>
> To illustrate this point, we might consider the record of Radio Corporation of America (RCA), the greatest glamour issue of the 1920s, and compare it with Syntex, a similar favorite of the post–World War II market.[9]

Comparison of RCA and Syntex Common Stocks for Selected Years[10]

Year	High RCA	Earnings (Share)	Year	High Syntex	Earnings (Share)
1925	77&7/8	$ 1.32	1962	11	$0.14
1926	61&5/8	2.85	1963	67&1/2	0.47
1927	101	6.15	1964	95&1/4	0.91
1928	420	15.98	1965	109	1.18

Both Trains were similar in nature and left the station with similar speed. It took *THE GREAT DEPRESSION* to derail Train #1. Train #2 is still on track.

Two points of view. Growth is reliably predictable. It is not.

The nature of the world does not change overnight. One of these views is closer to wrong, the other closer to right.

As we walk the tracks of the twentieth century, opinions *dramatically* cycle.

Heresy becomes truth.

Truth becomes heresy.

Heresy returns again as truth.

Which is which?

Let the evidence speak.

Notes

1. Although the following scenario is fictitious, the words of Edgar Lawrence Smith reflect his opinions, as stated in his book.

2. E. L. Smith, *Common Stocks as Long-Term Investments* (New York: Macmillan Company, 1925).

3. R. Sobel, *The Great Bull Market* (New York: W. W. Norton and Company, 1968), p. 119.

4. B. Graham and D. Dodd, *Security Analysis* (New York: McGraw-Hill, 1934), p. 314.

5. B. Graham, D. Dodd, and C. Tatham, *Security Analysis* (New York: McGraw-Hill, 1951).

6. W. B. Walker, *A Re-examination of Common Stocks as Long-Term Investments* (Portland, OR: Grand National Bank of Portland, 1954).

7. L. Fisher and J. Lorie, "Rates of Return on Investments in Common Stock," *Journal of Business* (January 1964).

8. M. J. Gordon, *The Investment, Financing and Valuation of the Corporation* (Homewood, IL: Richard D. Irwin, 1962), p. 5.

9. Sobel, *The Great Bull Market*, p. 122.

10. Ibid., p. 121.

CHAPTER 5

The Past and the Future

HIGGLEDY PIGGLEDY GROWTH

Ironically, just after Growth Train #2 pulled away from the station, a British economist named Little was immersed in research that would buttress the conservative views of the old timers.

I. M. D. Little.

(I'll leave it to you to figure out why Ian's parents thought he might need that third initial.)

Little was trying to determine whether the firms that grew the fastest in the past tended to repeat their relative performance in the future. In his writings, he repeatedly apologizes for even raising such a silly question. After all, isn't it obvious that the best firms of the past are, at the very least, going to be the better firms of the future?

Very much aware of the emergence of Train #2, Little writes in his 1962 article, "Higgledy Piggledy Growth":[1]

> My impression is that many stockholders, financial journalists, economists, and investors believe that past growth behavior is some sort of guide to future growth. This belief seems to have developed especially in the last few years.[2]

And in his 1966 book *Higgledy Piggledy Growth Again* with A. C. Rayner, they write:[3]

> Before launching into the investigation, it is well to start by giving some reasons for being interested in growth stability. The first is the one that the market is concerned with, which is that there has been, for the last few years, a belief in the concept of "growth stocks." For the privilege of holding these particular stocks, the investor has been willing to forgo a considerable amount of income in the belief that their market price will rise in the future. This can continue to happen in a rational market only if past growth is repeated in the future. Therefore, with this belief in growth stocks, investors are also expressing a belief that firms which have grown relatively better than others in the past will continue to do so in the future.[4]

Because the work in the *book* is more comprehensive, we will concentrate on *it*.

Rayner and Little (RL) study British companies over the period from 1951 through 1961.[5] Again, they were trying to determine whether growth in the past serves as a precursor for growth in the future.

In one of their tests, RL rank their firms based on their rates of growth in earnings per share from 1952 to 1956. They then form equal numbered groups, the fastest-growing firms, fast, slow, and slowest.

Each firm counts equally within a group. The earnings of each group are indexed where 1952 equals 100. We can see the growth of each group from 1952 to 1956 in Figure 5-1. The earnings of the fastest-growing firms move from 100 in 1952 to about 190 in 1956. The slowest fall to about 45.

The question of interest is: "Do the fastest continue to grow fast *after* the rankings are established in 1956? And do the slowest continue to grow slow?"

No.

From 1956 on, the growth performance of all four groups is about the same.

RL find no evidence in this test that the future is linked to the past—at least in terms of growth in earnings per share.

Okay, maybe across a wide variety of firms there is little or no consistency in relative performance, but what about among peers within an industry?

To find intra-industry consistency, RL rank firms in the same industry on the basis of growth in earnings per share in the first half of their period

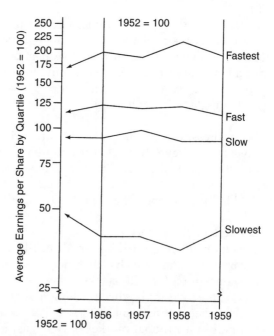

FIGURE 5-1 Earnings Behavior for Fastest-, Fast-, Slow-, and Slowest-Growing Firms (1952–56) *Source*: A. C. Rayner and I. M. D. Little, *Higgledy Riggledy Growth Again* (Oxford: Basil Blackwell, 1966), p. 22.

(roughly the first half of the 1950s), and then they rank them again in the second half. A firm's rank in the first half is plotted on the vertical axis of a graph, and the rank in the second half is on the horizontal. Each firm in their sample is represented as a dot on the graph. A firm ranking first in the first half and first in the second is positioned in the upper right-hand corner. A firm ranking last in both halves is positioned in the lower left-hand corner.

If the rankings are perfectly consistent from the first half of the decade to the second, all the dots should fall on a line going from the lower left corner to the upper right.

RL's results are presented in Figure 5-2.

Wow!

Shotgun blast!

RL run test after test trying to find some evidence of consistency in the record. They find none. Finally, they conclude:

> Certainly investors are wrong to think that a few years' above average rise of earnings is evidence at all that good management, which will result in a continued rise, must be present.[6]

Future growth as a *speculative* rather than an *investment* consideration.

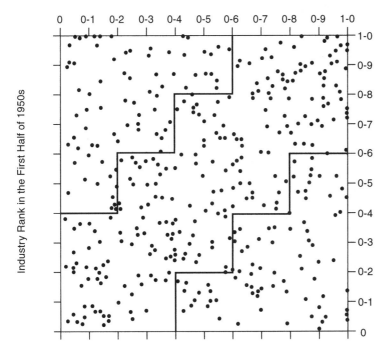

FIGURE 5-2 Consistency of Growth Relative to Other Firms in the Industry
Source: A. C. Rayner and I. M. D. Little, *Higgledy Piggledy Growth Again* (Oxford: Basil Blackwell, 1966), p. 50.

HIGGLEDY PIGGLEDY GROWTH IN AMERICA

The results of Little and Rayners' book and Little's article attracted much attention, at least in the academic community. Was this peculiar to the United Kingdom? Was it possible that relative growth was unpredictable in the United States as well?

Two professors from Harvard, John Lintner and Robert Glauber (LG), took a stab at that question.[7] (Lintner, you may recall, was one of the co-inventors of CAPM.)

LG look at five-year sub-periods within the period from 1946 through 1965.[8]

They are interested in explaining differences in growth in one period with differences in growth in the period that came before.

What percentage of the differences in growth across firms in one period can be associated with differences that were observed in the *preceding* period?

For RL's Figure 5-2, the answer to that question is close to zero. The rankings in the two periods are pretty much independent of one another. If, instead, the rankings were perfectly consistent (all dots on a straight line going from the southwest corner to the northeast), the answer would be 100%. All the growth differences in the second period could be associated with differences in the first.

LG conduct a similar analysis with U.S. firms.[9] However, in their study, *rates of growth* would be plotted on the axes of the graph rather than growth *rankings*.

Their results are presented in Figure 5-3.

The findings are very consistent with the results from the United Kingdom. At best, we can say that only 1.7% of the differences in growth rates

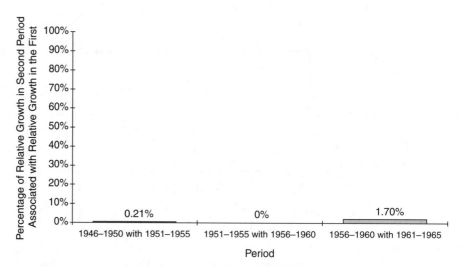

FIGURE 5-3 Percentage of Differential Earnings Growth in One Five-Year Period Associated with Earnings Growth in the Next Period *Source*: J. Lintner and R. Glauber, "Higgledy Piggledy Growth in America," (paper presented to the Seminar on the Analysis of Security Prices, University of Chicago, May 1967), Table 3, part (e).

in one five-year period (1961–65) can be associated with growth differences in the preceding period.

If you're trying to forecast which stocks are going to grow the fastest in the next five years, you can forget about using the last five years as a guide. The past is *not* a very good guide to the future.

But extrapolation of the past trend is at least the starting point of most contemporary professional forecasts of earnings per share.

FLIP FOR IT

So firms aren't very consistent when it comes to their growth rankings *per se*. Are they at least consistent when it comes to rougher measures of relative performance, such as being better or worse than average from year to year?

Another British professor, Richard Brealey, tried to find out.[10]

Brealey first ranks U.S. firms on the basis of their rate of growth in earnings per share.

Then he notes whether a particular firm is in the top or bottom half of the rankings from year to year.

Suppose, for a given firm over a period of years, we observe the following sequence of top halves (+) and bottom halves (−):

$$+ + - + - - + - + + + + - + - - -$$

Brealey now tabulates the number of runs he sees of various lengths. For example, for how many years do we see the firm staying on the top or bottom for a *single* year before switching to the opposite position?

Three + runs of length 1 and three −.

Now how many runs of length 2?

One + and one −.

And of lengths 3 and 4?

One − of length 3, and one + of length 4.

Brealey now runs this type of tabulation over all the firms in his sample.

But what if being in the top half or bottom half was simply a matter of luck?

We'll still see runs.

Flip a coin. If you're lucky, it won't take long before you flip five heads in a row. If you're flipping a fair coin, that's just a matter of luck.

However, count the number of runs in the win–loss records for the Los Angeles Lakers and the Boston Celtics and you *won't* conclude that success in basketball is just a matter of luck.

But what role does luck play in "winning" in terms of growth in earnings per share?

A graph of Brealey's tabulation is presented in Figures 5-4A and 5-4B. The length of run is plotted horizontally; the number of runs he sees is plotted vertically.

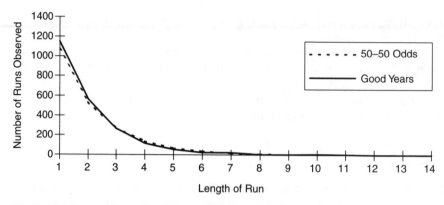

FIGURE 5-4A   Actual Number of Runs of Good Years versus 50-50 Odds

The broken curve shows the number of runs you'd expect to see if being above or below average in earnings growth were simply a matter of chance.

Simply a matter of flipping a fair coin.

Heads in the top half. Tails in the bottom.

The solid curves show the actual number of runs Brealey sees in his count.

Hard to tell the difference.

Note that we actually see more runs of short duration and fewer runs of long duration.

This is consistent with short-run inertia and long-run reversal patterns in the growth of *earnings per share.*

Do you remember?

In Chapter 2, we found these types of patterns in *rates of return to stocks.*

We seem to have a degree of corroboration here.

So far, however, the old timers seem to have the upper hand.

In fact, the old timers have gotten even more support from a recent study by Chan, Karceski, and Lakonishok (CKL).[11]

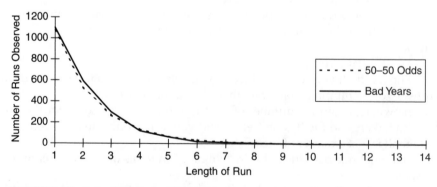

FIGURE 5-4B   Actual Number of Runs of Bad Years versus 50-50 Odds
Source: R. Brealey, *An Introduction to Risk and Return from Common Stocks*, 2nd ed. (Cambridge, MA: MIT Press, 1983).

They look at the period 1951–98. Their sample includes all U.S. firms on the New York, American, and Nasdaq markets. CKL are also looking at runs in above average growth in income before extraordinary items.

They slide a ten-year window through the period and test for runs within the moving window.

The solid line in Figure 5-5 shows the percentage of firms in their sample with successive years of above-average growth for runs of between one and ten years. The broken line shows the number of runs you would expect to see if, for each firm, the probability of being above average was 50% in each year.

Once again, we see an amazing consistency between records of success and pure chance.

THE CHRISTMAS TREE

Okay, so the past can't be counted on as a reliable guide to the future. The stocks that grew the fastest in the past can't be counted on to repeat their relative performance in the future. If you're going to make a forecast of the future relative rate of growth in earnings, you had better be prepared to base your projection on something other than a simple extrapolation of *past trend.*

However, those who forecast the future *can* base their forecasts on a rich variety of information in addition to a firm's *past* growth behavior.

Relevant information might include valuable patent rights, market leadership, recognizable brand name, strategic location, and astute management. These and many more can help a firm carve out a position that is conducive to rapid growth in future earnings per share.

Given its access to this type of information, how accurate are the *market's forecasts* of relative rates of growth in earnings?

Unfortunately, the market's expectations are not published anywhere, so we can't directly check their accuracy. However, there are indicators that can be used as signals of what the market is thinking.

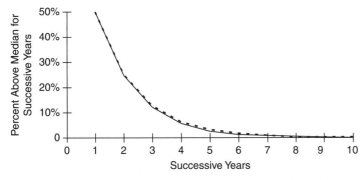

FIGURE 5-5   Consistency Between Records of Success and Pure Chance

As we discussed in Chapter 1, the market price of a stock reflects the market's assessment of its future prospects. It's likely to be the case that if the price is large relative to its accounting book value, the prospects are good. Conversely, a high book-to-price ratio would indicate that bad times are expected ahead.

The same is true for the relationship between market price and other accounting numbers such as earnings per share. If the price is large relative to current earnings, it is probably because the market is betting on *future* earnings being substantially larger than *current* earnings.

Stocks with low ratios of earnings-to-price tend to be growth stocks; stocks with high ratios tend to be value stocks.

But do growth stocks actually turn out to grow faster and value stocks slower than average?

In the *future? After* they have been identified as growth or value by the market?

Fuller, Huberts, and Levinson (FHL), three investment professionals, published an interesting study, which sheds a considerable amount of light on that question.[12]

At the end of March in each year, during the period from 1973 through 1990, FHL rank the firms in their study by the ratio of the previous year's earnings per share to market price per share.[13] (Presumably, by the end of March, the previous year's earnings would have been announced by their firms.) The 20% of the firms with the largest ratio (cheap value) go into the first group, the next 20% into the second group, down to the fifth group, which contains the 20% with the lowest ratio (expensive growth).[14] They then observe the relative rates of growth in earnings for each of the groups *in each of the next eight years.*[15]

Do the cheap value stocks actually turn out to grow more slowly than the expensive growth stocks?

If he were alive today, Benjamin Graham might be very surprised to hear that the answer to that question is actually *yes!*

The results of the test are presented in Figure 5-6. Relative growth is plotted horizontally as the difference between the growth of the groups with above or below average earnings-to-price ratios, relative to the growth of the middle 20% group. As we move up vertically, we move into the future relative to the year in which the stocks were originally ranked on the basis of their earnings-to-price ratios.

To illustrate, the firms with the highest ratios (cheap value) grew nearly 10% slower (0.3% versus 10.2%) than the middle group in the first year following the rankings. On the other hand, the firms with the lowest ratios (expensive growth) grew nearly 9% faster (18.8% versus 10.2%). It is also the case that the intermediate groups fall right where you'd expect them to be.

Some[16] have referred to this graph as the Christmas Tree, based on the presents I allege lie under its boughs.

This pattern persists in the second year following the ranking and in the third and the fourth, as well. The market, using whatever sources of information it sees fit, is able to clearly distinguish between the fast and slow growers for at least four years into the future.

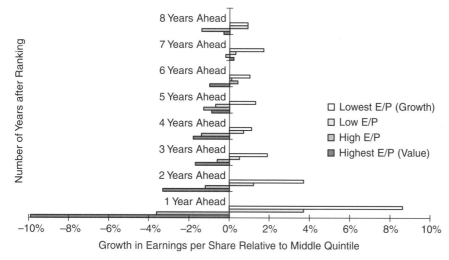

FIGURE 5-6 Relative Subsequent Growth in Highest, High, Low, and Lowest Quintiles of E/P Ratio *Source*: R. Fuller, L. Huberts, and M. Levinson, "Returns to E/P Strategies, Higgledy Piggledy Growth, Analysts' Forecast Errors, and Omitted Risk Factors," *Journal of Portfolio Management* (Winter 1993), Exhibit G.

How can we reconcile these results with the findings of Little, Rayner and Little, Lintner and Glauber, Brealey and Chan, Karceski and Lakonishok?

Keep in mind that most of the previous work observed the growth behavior of individual firms rather than large groups of stocks (like we're observing here). In addition, the previous work was directed at the relationship between past and future growth, as opposed to the relationship between the *structure of current market prices* and future growth. In setting prices, the market can take into account many factors in addition to past growth.

The results depicted in Figure 5-6 are still highly relevant because investors typically don't invest in *individual firms.* Rather, they invest (perhaps through mutual funds) in *large portfolios of many firms*, like the ones observed by FHL.

After seeing the results of their test, FHL conclude that (a) the results of earlier tests of "higgledy piggledy growth" were mistaken and (b) that the superlative performance of value-oriented stocks recorded by many, including themselves, is not due to the tendency of the market to overreact to a firm's past growth record. However, as stated previously, the earlier researchers were focusing on the relationship between the past and the future. FHL's results on the relationship between the levels of current stock prices and future growth don't show that the previous authors were mistaken about the missing link between the past and the future.

In addition, the issue is the *actual speed* of the reversion to the mean growth rate of the middle group, as evident in Figure 5-6, *relative to what was anticipated by the market* in setting the market prices for the stocks and the related ratios of earnings per share to market price.

The results of Figure 5-6 indicate that future growth pretty much reverts to the mean after five or six years. Was this what the market expected in setting the prices for the stocks in each group? *If you buy the growth stocks and their growth rates revert to the mean that quickly, what will the returns be on your investment in growth stocks relative to an investment in value stocks?*[17]

* * *

"Your Honor."

"Yes, Dr. Haugen."

"If the Court pleases, I would like to reserve the right to recall this exhibit later in these proceedings."

"We can't afford to waste time repeating ourselves, Dr. Haugen. Are you sure that a recall of this study will prove to be enlightening?"

"I am *quite* sure, Your Honor."

Notes

1. I. M. D. Little, "Higgledy Piggledy Growth," *Institute of Statistics Oxford* (November 1962).
2. Ibid., p. 391.
3. A. C. Rayner and I. M. D. Little, *Higgledy Piggledy Growth Again* (Oxford: Basil Blackwell, 1966).
4. Ibid., p. 1.
5. Their study includes 441 companies that had complete records through at least 1959.
6. Rayner and Little, *Higgledy Piggledy Growth Again*, p. 64.
7. J. Lintner and R. Glauber, "Higgledy Piggledy Growth in America" (paper presented to the Seminar on the Analysis of Security Prices, University of Chicago, May 1967).
8. Whereas RL measure growth by taking the ratio of ending to beginning earnings per share, LG fit a trend line through the natural logarithm of earnings plotted against time. They take the slope of the trend line as their measure of growth. This number can be taken to be the continuously compounded rate of growth, where beginning earnings are given by the level of the trend line at its starting point and ending earnings are given by its level at the ending point.
9. Their study covers 323 companies with positive earnings during the periods of analysis.
10. R. A. Brealey, *An Introduction to Risk and Return from Common Stocks* (Cambridge, MA: MIT Press, 1969).
11. K. C. Chan, J. Karceski, and J. Lakonishok, "The Level and Persistence of Growth Rates," *The Journal of Finance* (April 2003).
12. R. J. Fuller, L. C. Huberts, and M. J. Levinson, "Returns to E/P Strategies, Higgledy Piggledy Growth, Analysts' Forecast Errors, and Omitted Risk Factors," *The Journal of Portfolio Management* (Winter 1993).
13. To be included in their study, a firm must have had a total market capitalization (price per share times total number of common shares outstanding) equal to at least 0.01% of the total value of the S&P 500 stock index. The number of stocks included in their study ranged from 887 in 1973 to 1,179 in 1990.
14. The groups are industry diversified, in that each group contains 20% of the firms in a particular industry.
15. This process is repeated for as many years as their data would allow (from 1974 through 1992). Then the results are averaged across all the years.
16. The Ph.D. students in the finance seminar at Cal. Tech., upon studying the first draft of the first edition of this book. Aside to those students: "What do you think of the straw man now?"
17. As part of their study discussed above, CKL rank stocks on the basis of per-share growth rate in

income before extraordinary items over a sliding ten-year period. They form stocks into deciles with respect to this growth rate. They then look at the book-to-market ratio for the stocks at the beginning of each ten-year period (1951–98) to see if the market assigned lower ratios to the stocks that would actually grow the fastest over the subsequent ten years. Their results look like this:

Decile	1	2	3	4	5	6	7	8	9	10
Growth (%)	−18.9	−5.0	1.5	5.8	9.1	12.0	15.1	18.9	25.1	41.7
Beginning B/M	.653	.699	.696	.99	.726	.707	.723	.706	.742	.817

Based on the book-to-market ratios assigned to the stocks, it seems that the market was actually more optimistic about the stocks that were going to actually grow slowly during the next ten years at the beginning of the period.

CHAPTER 6

The Race Between Value and Growth

IN SEARCH OF MEDIOCRITY

Perhaps you have heard of the best-seller *In Search of Excellence: Lessons from America's Best-Run Corporations.*[1] The authors of this book took a list of companies considered to be innovative by a group of informed businesspeople and screened them on the following six measures of long-run financial superiority over the period 1961–1980:

1. Rate of growth in corporate assets
2. Rate of growth in book value
3. Average ratio of market price to book value
4. Average return on corporate assets[2]
5. Average return on book value
6. Average ratio of net income to sales

In studying the companies that passed the screening, the authors were able to identify the attributes that these companies seemed to have in common—the lessons.

In 1987, money manager Michelle Clayman published an article in which she tracked the performance of the stocks of these companies in the period following the ranking from 1981 through 1985.[3]

These firms had established strong records of performance prior to 1980. By 1980, they had become growth stocks. If the market overreacted and overpriced them, their performance after 1980 should be poor as the market corrects, and the prices of the stocks fall to more reasonable levels.

Clayman compares the performance of the "excellent" companies with another group that she calls "unexcellent." These were the 39 companies in the S&P 500 population that had the *worst* combination of the six characteristics as of the end of 1980 (cheap value stocks).

A comparison of the excellent and the unexcellent, in terms of the six characteristics, can be seen in Figure 6-1. As you can see, the bad are truly bad: slow rates of growth, low market to book, and suffering *losses* in income available to stockholders.

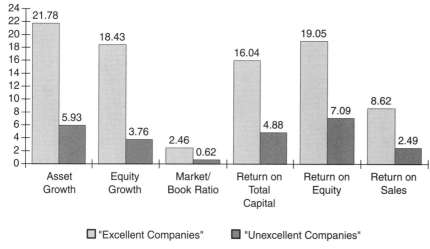

FIGURE 6-1 Characteristics of "Excellent" and "Unexcellent" Companies (1976–80)
Source: M. Clayman, "In Search of Excellence: The Investor's Viewpoint," *Financial Analysts Journal* (1987), Figure B, p. 58.

But Clayman reveals that the stunning characteristics of the excellent companies quickly reverted toward the mean in the years that followed their 1980 screening. Rates of growth in assets and book value nearly halved. Significant reductions were experienced in the other four categories as well.

As I. M. D. Little and others discovered, it is difficult to remain outstanding in a competitive world for very long.

The un-excellent companies also reverted toward the mean. They showed substantial improvement in their median values for all six categories.[4]

Once again, the market didn't anticipate the speed of the mean reversion.

The relative performance of the two groups of companies is presented in Figure 6-2.

Value wins.

The book *In Search of Excellence* may well be quite valuable to the prospective managers of innovative firms, but the successful investor should look more favorably on those firms that have been the mirror images *in the past* of those touted in the book.

REMOVING THE SIZE EFFECT FROM GO

Growth stocks tend to be large companies. Value stocks tend to be small companies.

Growth stocks will constitute a larger fraction of the total market value–weighted S&P 500 than will value stocks.

The S&P 500 stock index is heavily invested in expensive growth stocks.

Interesting.

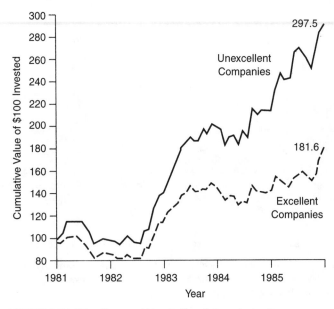

FIGURE 6-2 "Excellent and Unexcellent" Cumulative Return 1981–85 *Source*: M. Clayman, "In Search of Excellence: The Investor's Viewpoint," *Financial Analysts Journal* (1987), p. 63.

Many pension funds and other institutional investors like to invest large chunks of their money in portfolios that replicate the composition of the S&P. They call this strategy *indexing*.

Based on what we are seeing, indexing doesn't seem to be a very smart move on their part.

These results show that GO is clearly a valuable strategy in the long run, but how reliable is it in the short run?

After all, if it doesn't work for a while, some of us may panic and give up.

Fortunately for the impatient, it's pretty reliable—at least over five to ten-year periods.[5]

Even if you're prone to panic, if you can hold out for five or ten years, you're highly likely to see GO smile upon you.

Regardless of their cheapness characteristics, small stocks have tended to produce greater than average rates of return over the long run.

This may be because investors consider them to be (a) riskier or (b) more costly to trade. Information about the nature and activities of small stocks is scarcer. They are also less actively traded, so dealers may establish a larger spread between the price they are willing to buy and the price they are willing to sell, so they can make a decent "buck" while making a market for the stocks.

For whatever reason, for long periods of time (at least since 1926), they have tended to produce higher rates of return.

We now know that cheap value stocks *tend* to be small stocks.

This means that *a part* of GO is not the result of market overreaction, but rather, simply the result of investing in small stocks.

How much?

Three professors named Lakonishok, Shleifer, and Vishny (LSV) attempted to find out.[6] LSV also rank stocks by book to market. They then form portfolios. The 10% of the stocks with the largest ratio of book to market go into portfolio #1, the next 10% into portfolio #2, and so on. The portfolios are reformed annually, and their performance is observed over the next five years *on a buy and hold basis.* This process begins in 1968–72 and continues through the final five-year period, 1985–89.

LSV adjust the returns for size by subtracting from the monthly return of each stock, the monthly return from a portfolio of comparable size. In an overreactive market, cheap stocks should outperform other stocks in their size class, and expensive stocks should underperform.

We see that this is indeed the case in Figure 6-3 in which we plot the average annual over- or underperformance across all of their five-year periods.

In the extreme groupings, the cheapest stocks are out-performing by about 3.5%, and the most expensive stocks are underperforming by more than 4%.

Note that once again performance falls steadily and reliably as we move from cheap to expensive.

The average size (market price per share times number of shares) is also listed in Figure 6-3, so, once again, you can see that the expensive stocks tend to be larger companies.

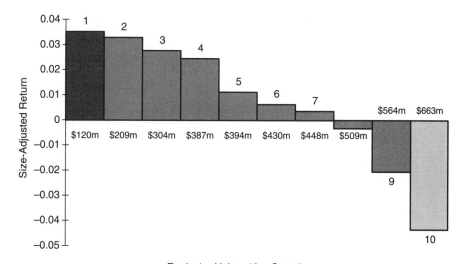

Rank; 1 = Value, 10 = Growth

FIGURE 6-3 Size-Adjusted Returns to Value and Growth *Source*: J. Lakonishok, A. Schleifer, and R. Vishney, "Contrarian Investment, Extrapolation and Risk," *The Journal of Finance* (1994).

GOING AROUND THE WORLD

Human behavior is human behavior, wherever we live. Moreover, although it has lost its position at the head of the pack in some areas, as evidenced by the global economic crisis of '08-09, *the United States is still the world's leader in finance.* If we embrace investment styles like expensive growth stocks, the rest of the world will do so also.

Overreacting is catchy.

Fama and French (FF) recently conducted a study of 14 foreign countries to see how value stocks perform relative to growth stocks throughout the world.[7]

FF use a database that is free from survival bias and which contains data that had been actually reported at the end of each month in their study. The stocks in their study represent approximately 80% of the total market value of all the stocks in the 13 countries. The period covered was from January 1975 through December 2004. FF combine stocks across the 14 countries and then rank stocks in each country at the end of each year by the ratio of the most recently available book value to the year-end market price of each stock. They then form five quintile portfolios, each containing 20% of the stocks and each weighted on the basis of the total market value of each stock. The stocks are re-ranked and the portfolios are reformed each year.

Figure 6-4 shows the average annualized returns to each group.

On average value outperforms growth in the foreign countries by 10.85%.

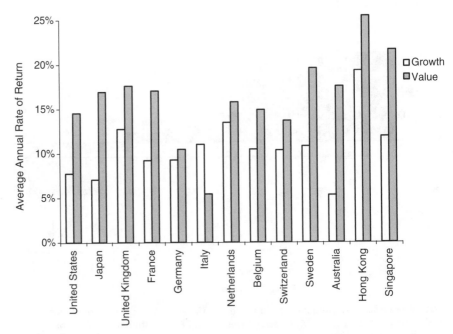

FIGURE 6-4   The Value Effect in International Stocks   *Source*: E. Fama and K. French, "The Value Premium and the CAPM," *The Journal of Finance* (2006), pp. 2163–2186.

By now it should be evident that what we have seen in the U.S. data is not a fluke, but rather a phenomenon of fundamental importance that we should be prepared to take advantage of.

THE LONG-TERM RACE BETWEEN VALUE AND GROWTH

In Chapter 4 we learned that, after a brief flirtation with growth stock investing that occurred in the late 1920s, growth stocks were "out of fashion" until the early 1960s. Rather, serious investors followed the many editions of the bible that was written by Graham and Dodd. Their central theme was to always value stocks based on current normalized earnings. Relative future growth was to play no role in stock valuation. The wisdom of this advice was evident in the results presented in Chapter 5. During this time, stocks should have been priced fairly with respect to their true underlying growth prospects, and we would expect the outcome in the race between value and growth to be a tie.

The international results presented above are actually only a part of a larger study by FF, which concentrates on the United States for the most part. Their study includes nearly 3,900 U.S. stocks. As in their earlier study, discussed in Chapter 1, stocks are ranked by book-to-market as of the end of June of each year.

The risk-adjusted (using The Theory) average *monthly* returns to stock portfolios classified as small value, small growth, large value, and large growth by FF are presented below. The results for the era of Graham and Dodd (where growth stocks didn't exist) are presented in Figure 6-5A, and the results for the extended modern period of growth stock investing are presented in Figure 6-5B.

Ah Hah!

These are exactly the results we would expect to see. There is no statistically significant difference between the growth and value returns in the Graham and Dodd era. Remember, Graham and Dodd believed that valuation should not reflect expectations of future growth in earnings per share. However, the difference between value and growth is *overwhelmingly* significant in the modern era of growth stock investing, when stock market prices include an unwarranted premium for *anticipated* growth.

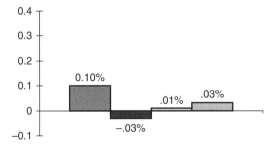

FIGURE 6-5A   July 1930 through June 1963 (Era of Graham and Dodd)

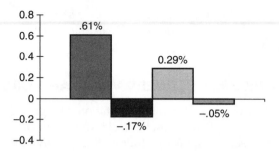

FIGURE 6-5B July 1963 through December 2004 (Era of modern growth stock investing) *Source*: E. Fama and K. French, "The Value Premium and the CAPM," *The Journal of Finance* (2006).

Notes

1. T. J. Peters and R. H. Waterman, *In Search of Excellence: Lessons from America's Best-Run Corporations* (New York: Harper & Row, 1982).

2. Return on total assets was measured by net income divided by the aggregate of long-term debt, preferred stock, and book value of common equity.

3. M. Clayman, "In Search of Excellence: The Investors Viewpoint," *Financial Analysts Journal* (May–June 1987).

4. In *The Inefficient Stock Market—What Pays Off and Why* (Upper Saddle River, NJ: Prentice Hall, 1998), and here in chapter 10 I argue that the payoff to profitability is positive. This would seem to contradict Clayman's results. However, what I argue is that, *holding the price you pay for a stock constant,* the more profitable the company, the better the outlook for future return. Clayman's unexcellent companies are both unprofitable and cheap (high book-to-price ratio).

5. This is probably too long to wait for most pension funds, which is why so many feel more comfortable with indexing.

6. J. Lakonishok, A. Schleifer, and R. Vishny, "Contrarian Investment, Extrapolation and Risk," *Journal of Finance* (December 1994).

7. E. Fama and K. French, "The Value Premium and the CAPM," *Journal of Finance* (October 2006).

CHAPTER 7

Surprise or Risk Premium?

THE DEBATE OVER THE NATURE OF GO

Even the Zealots, who still cling tenaciously to the tenets of market efficiency, believe that *The Theory (CAPM)* must go.

They have seen and have verified that GO (Golden Opportunity) exists. Many others[1] had reported the existence of GO decades before, but the Zealots scoffed at these early primitive "fossils" because they believed the methods used to measure the performance of cheap value strategies was flawed.

The reason the Fama and French study of Chapter 1 made headlines was that Fama, a long-time champion of CAPM *(The Theory)* and market efficiency *(The Fantasy)*, was one of the authors.

The *"Pope" said God was dead.*[2]

At least the god of *CAPM.*

The god of *The Fantasy* was, apparently, very much alive.

But how to explain GO? How to explain the premium to value investing?

Aha! What we've got here is a *risk* premium.

It's *not* the artifact of corrected overreaction. It's *not* a surprise.

You see, the Zealots believe that everyone knows, and has known all along, about GO. Everyone knows you can get to Diamond Head by investing in value stocks. However, we're not packing our bags because it seems that, for many, the trip doesn't have much appeal.

Let The Fantasy speak:

"It seems that cheap stocks have low current prices and high future returns because they are *risky.*"[3]

And just, why are value stocks supposedly more risky in the first place?

According to the latest versions of The Fantasy, value stocks are "Fallen Angels"—the stocks of once successful companies whose fortunes have long since turned against them.

They've been beaten up so badly that they now *scare the daylights out of us!*

In fact they scare us so much that many of us refuse to invest in them even though we believe that doing so will ultimately take us all the way to Diamond Head. People are so scared that they willingly shun Diamond Head (retiring at roughly $280,000 per year) and set their sights on Diamond Bar (roughly $2,700 per year) instead.

Yes, we *knowingly* and *willingly* pick Diamond *Bar*. So says The Fantasy.

The Fallen Angels must be scary indeed!

But wait a minute. Remember Figure 1-3? According to FF, value stocks have lower risk.

So what's to be scared about?

Whatever's supposed to be scaring us apparently isn't showing up in instability of the prices of cheap stocks.

Most of the time stock prices change because of the arrival of new information.

What's scaring us won't show up in price instability if we don't periodically hear new things about it.

There's a monster sleeping under your bed. It scares the living daylights out of you, but it's sleeping. Your bedroom is, and has been, very quiet. Makes no difference. You're still scared.

Cheap stocks might be plagued by *sleeping monsters.*

The problem with this story is that we need many different types of monsters because there are many different kinds of value stocks breeding in many different types of industries.

And it's hard to come up with all these monster stories.

Moreover, it's been shown that GO is an intra-industry effect and not an inter-industry effect.[4] We apparently don't see a value premium in going from one industry to the next. The premium lies *within* each industry in going from one stock to the next.

Believers in The Fantasy have a really tough job ahead of them.

And what about the expensive growth stocks? The Fantasy says that we know that they will have low returns. We know that they will take us to Diamond *Bar*. We go anyway because we are allegedly so *fond of the ride.*

But why aren't we afraid of the many bumps along the way? Why aren't we concerned about the volatility that we see in them in Figure 1-3? What's going to save us? Who will ultimately show up to rescue us from the wild swings in our performance to make us confident that we will eventually end up at Diamond *Bar*.

Silent Angels?

LEARNING HOW TO MAKE GO DISAPPEAR

Fama and French (FF) admit that the premium to value investing is *real* and not merely a statistical artifact.

However, in keeping with their fervent belief in The Fantasy, they claim that the premium will disappear *if the returns to the groups are properly risk adjusted.*

So, in most of their works, FF risk adjust the returns to growth and value portfolios. They do this with a clever statistical manipulation. They regress monthly stock portfolio returns (in excess of the T-bill rate) on (a) the returns to the S&P 500 (in excess of the T-bill rate), (b) the difference between the returns on large and small stocks, and (c) *on the difference between the returns to value and growth stock* portfolios. They then take the intercept obtained by performing this regression on any given class of stocks as a measure of risk-adjusted return. As any statistician will tell you, the intercept of this regression is actually the expected return to the group conditional on a specific market environment. In this market environment (a) the stock market index produces a return equal to the T-bill rate, (b) small stocks on average produce returns equal to the average return produced by large stocks and (c) *value stocks on average produce returns equal to the average of growth stocks.*

FF find that the "risk-adjusted" intercepts for value and growth are not significantly different from one another. They then ascribe the difference in the *raw returns* to a risk premium.

Just what does this mean anyway?

It means *this.*

And *only* this.

In market environments during which value does not outperform growth, the returns to value and growth should not be significantly different from one another.

And just what are we supposed to make of this statement (which is true by definition)?[5]

In spite of the fact that the FF risk-adjustment process seems to be meaningless and self-fulfilling, the procedure seems to have developed a wide following among their academic disciples. Most disciples are now compelled to use it to "properly" risk adjust the returns in their studies "verifying" the efficient market.

Many find they must "risk adjust" using more than three factors. You see, it depends on how many anomalies they are trying to "get rid of." Consider the evidence of momentum in stock returns discovered by Jegadeesh and Titman as discussed in Chapter 3. If you want to eliminate the momentum premium in stock returns, simply add a factor equal to the monthly difference in the returns to winning and losing firms over the interval in which you find momentum and voila! You will find there's no significant difference between the returns to portfolios of winners and losers in market environments in which the performance of both is the same.

As a matter of fact, I am so impressed by the *robust* character of this flexible, ad hoc, multifactor, risk-adjustment process devised by FF that I propose it take its proper place on a solid gold pedestal beside the hallowed Preposterous Private Information Hypothesis,[6] which itself resides securely in the Great Hall of Divine Saviors at the Holy Temple of Efficient Markets.

Servatorem meum in basem auream pono, in magnoatrio Servatorum.

WHEN WE GO TO DIAMOND HEAD

There is another problem with The Fantasy's risk premium story.

If GO really represents the delivery of a risk premium, it should be earned pretty uniformly through time. At least with the same uniformity that investors are *exposed* and *sensitized* to risk.[7]

However, we learned from Figure 3-1A and 3-1B that a *big* chunk of GO comes at the three-day window of time *when firms announce their earnings.* We

Heretics claim that the market is being caught by surprise—expensive stocks reporting unexpectedly bad earnings and cheap stocks unexpectedly good.

Believers in The Fantasy must argue that risk is especially high during these periods, and the relatively high returns to cheap stocks are risk premiums being earned as the risk is experienced. *But the Zealots must come up with believable explanations for the following observations* for the earnings announcement dates:

a. Why does the uncertainty initially go up for the winners (and presumably more expensive) stocks, which generally produce high returns around earnings announcements and down for the losing, cheap stocks, for which returns are low?

b. Why does the relative risk switch around (as we see in Figure 3-1A and 3-1B) after the eighth month following rankings of performance over the previous six months? We have argued that, initially, the inefficient market fails to recognize a good report as a precursor of a few more to follow. When the good reports come, it overreacts, thinking the string of good reports will continue unabated for a long period into the future. But can the Zealots explain the switch in terms of shifts in relative risk?

And here's a result that should prove even more puzzling to believers in The Fantasy.

Three more professors, Chopra, Lakonishok, and Ritter (CLR), find that the rest of GO comes at *the turn of the year.*[8]

CLR rank the stocks in their study on the basis of the return over the previous five years.[9] They put the 5% of the stocks with the worst trailing five-year records into group 1, the 5% with the second worst into group 2, and so on through group 20, the winners.

The average monthly return to these stocks during the five years *after they are ranked* is plotted in Figure 7-1. The monthly average returns in January are shown in the rear, and the average returns for the other months are shown in the front.[10]

Incredible!

The past losers produce *huge* January returns relative to the past winners.[11] Why?

This is not an especially risky period for the cheap, losing stocks. Nor is it an especially safe one for the expensive, winning stocks.

It is, however, an especially active period for many money managers.

Managers who have done well during the year have an incentive to lock in their performance as they approach the winter months. Bonuses don't increase much when great performance becomes really great, but they shrink dramatically if great becomes mediocre.

So if you've done great, lock your performance in. How? You are probably benchmarked relative to the S&P 500 index. As you liquidate your profitable aggressive positions, park the proceeds in blue-chip stocks that behave like your benchmark.

Same thing if you're doing really badly. Lock out disaster by selling off the sour notes. Replace them with blue chips that will look good to your clients

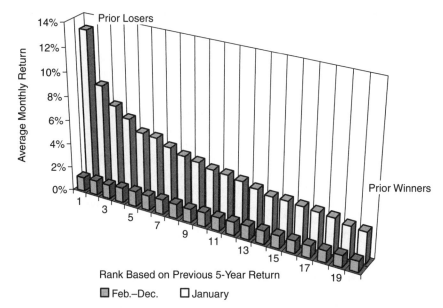

FIGURE 7-1 Seasonal Returns to Value and Growth Portfolios *Source*: N. Chopra, J. Lakonishok, and J. Ritter, "Measuring Abnormal Performance: Do Stocks Overreact?" *Journal of Financial Economics* 31, no. 2 (April 1992), Table 3.

when they inspect the portfolio at the end of the year. By investing in blue-chip stocks, which make up a big part of your benchmark for the remainder of the year, you keep your relative performance out of the disaster zone.

The process of locking in good performance and locking out disaster takes place at different times for different managers during the later part of the year. So the process of exiting from aggressive positions can be expected to have little market impact.

Going back, however, is a different story.

On the morning of the first trading day of the year, the starter's gun is raised into the air and fired.

The race to beat the market is *on* for a fresh calendar year.

The pros who previously locked in or out simultaneously move back.

But they move back selectively, looking to buy the stocks they believe are undervalued. Looking for bargains. Stocks that have been driven down too far. Looking to avoid or sell short stocks that are overvalued. Stocks selling at bloated prices.

Because the pros all move at once, their trades bump stock prices, pushing the bargains up and the bloated down.

What we're seeing in Figure 7-1 is not the delivery of a risk premium. There is nothing especially risky about the month of January. Instead, we're seeing the tracks of stocks being pushed back by professional investors to fair values.

Stocks that had been over or undervalued by an overreactive market.

GO is *not* a risk premium expected by a rational and efficient market.

It is a *surprise*.[12]

Notes

1. See, for example, S. Basu, "The Investment Performance of Common Stocks in Relation to Their Price-Earnings Ratios," *Journal of Finance* (June 1977); S. Basu, "The Relationship Between Earnings Yield, Market Value and Return for NYSE Common Stocks," *Journal of Financial Economics* (June 1983); W. Breen, "Low Price-Earnings Ratios and Industry Relatives," *Financial Analysts Journal* (July–August 1968); S. Huang, "Study of the Performance of Rapid Growth Stocks," *Financial Analysts Journal* (January–February 1965); F. K. Flugel, "The Rate of Return on High and Low P/E Ratio Stocks," *Financial Analysts Journal* (November–December 1968).

2. On April 16, 1998, at the UCLA conference "The Market Efficiency Debate: A Break from Tradition," while delivering a paper on market efficiency, Fama said that he believed that *God* knew that the stock market was efficient. He added that the closer one came to Behavioral Finance, the hotter one could feel the fires of Hell on one's feet. As we shall see in Chapter 12, it is likely that The New Finance resides much closer to Hell than Behavioral Finance. **Ouch!**

3. In J. Lakonishok, A. Shleifer, and R. Vishny, "Contrarian Investment, Extrapolation and Risk," *Journal of Finance* (December 1994), value stocks are found to outperform the market index on average over the index's worst 25 months of performance, over the best 25 months of performance, over the negative performance months, and over the positive performance months (see their Table 7).

4. See S. P. Kothari, J. Shanken, and R. G. Sloan, "Another Look at the Cross-Section of Stock Returns," *Journal of Finance* (March 1995). In this paper, they find that GO tends to disappear when cap-weighted industry indexes are ranked rather than individual firms. The authors contend that the industry indexes suffer less from survival bias problems. However, the clear presence of GO in studies commencing after 1980 as well as its presence in studies presented in the next chapter that are cleaned of survival bias indicates that its disappearance in an industry study is due to something else. Many industries are dominated by one or two relatively large firms. *To the extent that GO is a minor factor for the largest firms, it is likely to disappear when cap-weighted industry indexes are used to find it.* Moreover, it is likely that differences in book-to-market ratios across industries are more related to differences in capital requirements for production than to relative cheapness in stock prices.

5. In K. Daniel and S. Titman, "Evidence on the Characteristics of Cross-Sectional Variation in Stock Returns," *Journal of Finance* (1997), it is shown that, while cheap stocks do have higher returns, stocks that have higher levels of correlation with the FF value/growth factor do not tend to have higher returns. This casts more doubt on the proposition that a stock's beta relative to the book/market factor can be taken as a measure of risk.

6. See K. French and R. Roll, "Stock Return Variances: The Arrival of Information and the Reaction of Traders," *Journal of Financial Economics* (1986). French and Roll (FR) find that on those Wednesdays in 1968 when the New York Stock Exchange closed to catch up on paperwork, the volatility of stock prices was a tiny fraction of its value when the exchange was open. During the hours of normal trading on those Wednesdays, all other sources of information relevant to the pricing of stocks were going full blast. The only source of information shut down was the changes in the prices of the stocks themselves. Rather than come to the obvious conclusion that a major component of stock volatility is driven by reactions to changes in stock prices (a conclusion that would be inconsistent with efficient markets), FR conclude that possibly investors stop looking for new information when the market is closed because they must wait until the market is open to act on it. In *Beast on Wall Street*, I refer to this as the Preposterous Private Information Hypothesis. As I argue in Chapter 11 of this book, the source of the extra volatility when the exchange is open is the complex and even chaotic inter-action of traders as they respond to reported changes in the prices of shares and changes in their estimates of market risk.

7. Not only is it possible that the level of risk changes over time, but it is also possible that the level of risk aversion change as we go through different points in the business cycle in which investors earn different levels of income.

8. N. Chopra, J. Lakonishok, and J. Ritter, "Measuring Abnormal Performance," *Journal of Financial Economics* (April 1992), p. 235.

9. CLR look at New York Stock Exchange firms over the period from 1926 through 1986. The results of Figure 7-1 reflect averages of five-year windows of time over this entire period.

10. CLR also find that a large chunk of GO comes in three-day windows around earnings announcement days. Their results are similar to those of Jegadeesh and Titman (Figure 3-1A and 3-1B), except that CLR initially rank stocks on the basis of their total returns over the past *five years* rather than the *six-month* period used by JT. Because they rank on the basis of the longer period, they find evidence of the long-term reversal pattern, but they fail to detect the short-term inertia pattern in returns.

11. This result was discovered first by W. DeBondt and R. Thaler, "Does the Stock Market Overreact?" *Journal of Finance* (July 1985).

12. In yet another paper (E. F. Fama and K. R. French, "Common Risk Factors in the Returns on Stocks and Bonds," *Journal of Financial Economics* [February 1993], FF show (Table 9a, Panel iv) that in market environments in which (a) the performance of high and low book/price stocks are equal, (b) the performance of large and small stocks are equal, and (c) the broad market index produces a return equal to the risk-free rate, we should not expect to see any of the size or book/price based quintiles outperforming. This, of course, is not very convincing to the Heretics. They want proof that the road to Diamond Head is fraught with perils. They also want to know why the premium to value is delivered with such a peculiar seasonal pattern—a pattern that fits nicely with the overreactive market hypothesis. *It is not sufficient to merely call the premium to value investing a risk premium.*

CHAPTER 8

"Bearing" Risk in the Stock Market

ONE-MONTH HORIZON TESTS OF THE RELATIONSHIP BETWEEN RISK AND EXPECTED RETURN

Let's recap some of the things we've learned so far:

a. Cheap stocks tend to produce higher returns; expensive stocks tend to produce lower returns.

b. Cheap stocks tend to be less risky; expensive stocks tend to be more risky.

   Given (a) and (b), it would seem to be the case that:

c. *Low-risk stocks have high expected returns; high-risk stocks have low expected returns.*

But a typical MBA will tell you: "In the stock market, risk and return are *positively* related—the greater the risk, the greater the expected return."

That's because the MBA was carefully trained to believe in both The Theory and The Fantasy.

Although Fama and French (FF) do not *admit* that (c) is evident in their results, a closer look reveals that it is.

In Figures 8-1A through Figure 8-1J, we plot the relationship between risk (beta) and realized return for the ten size groupings (Figure 8-1A the smallest stocks, Figure 8-1J the largest) analyzed by FF.[1] We have drawn standard regression lines[2] through each of the scatter plots. *All of the lines have negative slopes*, although all are not significantly negative.

In a more recent study[3] Ang, Hodrick, Xing, and Zhang (AHXZ) find a negative relationship between average stock return and the component of a stock's volatility that cannot be explained by the three "risk adjustment" factors of FF—excess market return, the difference in the returns of big and small stocks, and the difference in the value and growth of stocks. Let's call this unexplained component of volatility *residual volatility*.

At the beginning of each month in the period July 1963 through December 2000, AHXZ rank stocks on the basis of residual volatility, computed using daily returns for the previous month. They then form five portfolios based on these rankings, each with an equal total market value. Each of the portfolios is weighted on the basis of the total market value

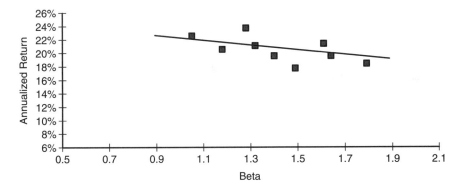

FIGURE 8-1A A Test of the Risk–Return Relationship Using One-Month Horizon: Decile 1 (1963–90)

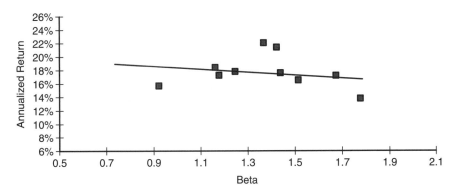

FIGURE 8-1B A Test of the Risk–Return Relationship Using One-Month Horizon: Decile 2 (1963–90)

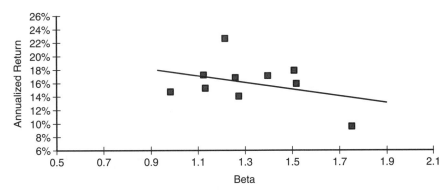

FIGURE 8-1C A Test of the Risk–Return Relationship Using One-Month Horizon: Decile 3 (1963–90)

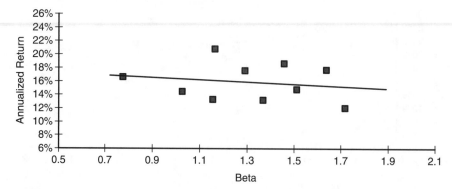

FIGURE 8-1D A Test of the Risk–Return Relationship Using One-Month Horizon: Decile 4 (1963–90)

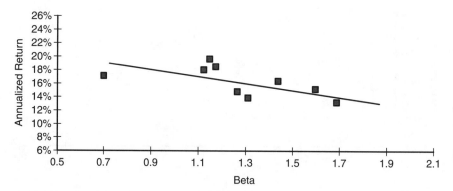

FIGURE 8-1E A Test of the Risk–Return Relationship Using One-Month Horizon: Decile 5 (1963–90)

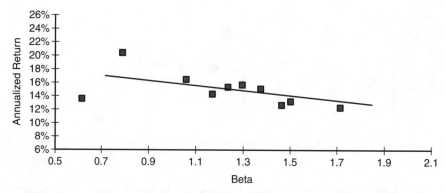

FIGURE 8-1F A Test of the Risk–Return Relationship Using One-Month Horizon: Decile 6 (1963–90)

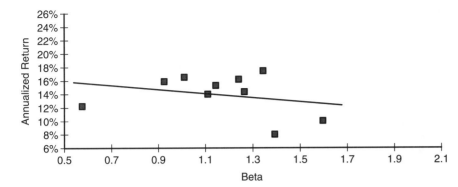

FIGURE 8-1G   A Test of the Risk–Return Relationship Using One-Month Horizon: Decile 7
(1963–90)

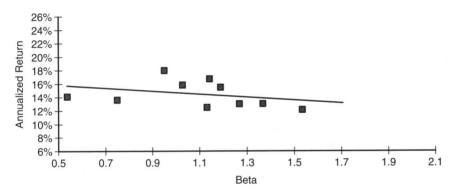

FIGURE 8-1H   A Test of the Risk–Return Relationship Using One-Month Horizon: Decile 8
(1963–90)

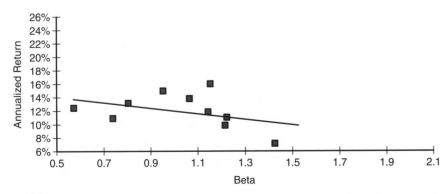

FIGURE 8-1I   A Test of the Risk–Return Relationship Using One-Month Horizon: Decile 9
(1963–90)

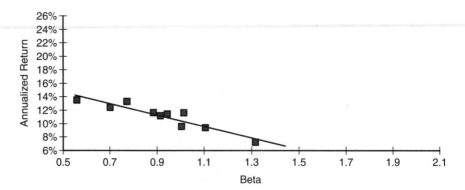

FIGURE 8-1J   A Test of the Risk–Return Relationship Using One-Month Horizon: Decile 10 (1963–90)   *Source*: E. Fama and K. French, "The Cross-Section of Expected Stock Returns," *Journal of Finance* 47, no. 2 (June 1992), Table I.

of each stock. The average annualized returns to the portfolios are plotted in Figure 8-2.

The difference in average return between the lowest-and highest-risk portfolio is highly statistically significant. AHXZ estimate that the price of risk is negative *after 1963*.

As we show in the appendix to this chapter, the relationship between risk and return found in the results of FF and AHXZ would have been even more significant had a proper measure of return been employed.

THE HERETICS AND THE ZEALOTS FINALLY AGREE

Both the Heretics and the Zealots agree that The Theory should be abandoned. Both see the premium returns in value investing. The disagreement is over the nature of the premium—is it a surprise or a risk premium?

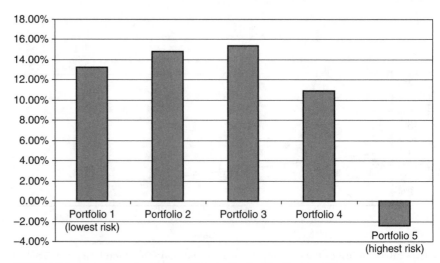

FIGURE 8-2   Returns to Portfolios of Stocks Ranked by Residual Risk

Both would agree that The Theory is wrong about the major market indexes being positioned in the vicinity of the efficient set. Both would agree that portfolios with lower volatility and higher return are attainable.

The argument centers on the *nature* of GO. Is it a *surprise* or is it a *risk premium*?

The Zealots argue that the premium to low-volatility portfolios stems from the fact that risk has a deeper meaning to investors. Risk goes beyond volatility to the sensitivity of returns to a multiplicity of macroeconomic factors. Concern over these "higher" dimensions of risk transcends concerns about volatility.

There's something about the low-volatility portfolios that frightens us. There's something about the high-volatility portfolios that gives us comfort. We *expect* and *require* the differential returns on these portfolios.[4]

So they say.

It's not mispricing stemming from overreaction that creates systematic and predictable differences between what is *expected* and what is ultimately *received*. A pattern of mispricing that overrides our desire to get higher returns from high-volatility investments.

But we say.

We *want* higher returns on high-volatility stock portfolios, but we don't *get* them because we overreact to the past and ultimately receive low returns to the more volatile growth stocks in the future.

We are afraid of volatility. We are *very* afraid.

This is why Edgar Lawrence Smith and many others find that stocks consistently outstrip bonds in their returns by such a wide margin. Stocks as a class *do* carry a risk premium—a big one. And we see evidence of it again and again. It's hard to find ten-year periods where bonds outperform stocks. The risk premium in expected aggregate stock returns manifests itself again and again in the realized differential returns between stocks and bonds.

But what about the risk premium in the *cross section* of stock returns? Why don't we see the risk premium in expected stock returns manifest itself in realized returns?

Because it's simply not there.

You see, we *are* afraid of stock volatility, and we *do* demand very high returns to invest in stocks.

Our fear can also be seen in studies that transcend the cross-sectional distortion in relative stock prices caused by overreaction. These studies, including the evidence provided by Figure 11-2A in this book, document the fact that we react very negatively to unexpected increases in the *overall* level of volatility in the market.[5,6]

As the volatility of the market index goes up, the *general level* of stock prices goes down so that higher returns can be earned in the future as we go through the period of higher volatility. And the returns do turn out to be higher, *following* the price adjustment.

Conversely, unexpected drops in volatility are accompanied by increases in the level of stock prices as investors lower their required returns. And realized returns turn out to be relatively low following the price adjustment.

Our reactions to changes in volatility are strong, consistent, and significant. We *are* afraid of volatility.

But these fears don't show up in the cross section of stock returns, because our expectations are blurred and ultimately erased by market price distortions related to overreaction.[7]

WHY YOU DON'T SEE THIS IN THE TEXTBOOKS

Maybe you have seen graphs in finance books showing a positive relationship between risk and expected return in the stock market.

Where did these results come from? Did somebody make them up?

To see what's been fooling us for so long, we need to go back to the FF study of Chapter 1.

FF did some tests that extended over a long period (1941–90). In these tests, NYSE stocks were ranked first by size during each year. The largest 10% of the stocks went into group 1, the next largest 10% into group 2, and so on. In each successive year the stocks were re-ranked and regrouped.[8]

Then the monthly returns to each of the groups are observed over the period from 1941 to 1990. The average returns to each group are plotted against their market sensitivity (beta) in Figure 8-3A. The smallest stocks are to the upper right, and the stocks become progressively larger as we move to the lower left.

We see a positive trade-off between risk and realized return.

This is what you're used to seeing.

But what we're seeing here is not a manifestation of a *risk premium*. It is, in fact, a manifestation of a *size or liquidity premium*. Small stocks carry bigger expected returns. They also tend to be riskier. But their superior returns are driven by size and the higher associated costs of trading these stocks rather than by their greater market risk.

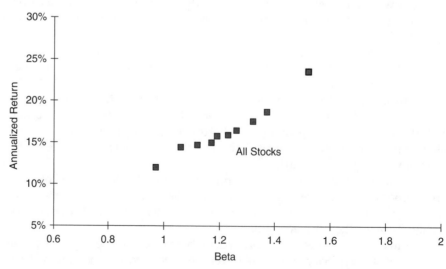

FIGURE 8-3A   Beta versus Return for Size-Formed Portfolios (NYSE 1941–90)

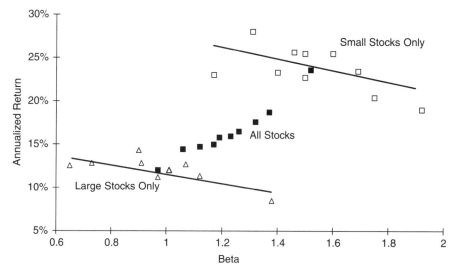

FIGURE 8-3B   Beta versus Return for Large and Small Stocks (NYSE 1941–90)
Source: E. Fama and K. French, "The Cross-Section of Expected Stock Returns," *Journal of Finance* 47, no. 2 (June 1992), Table A.II.

To show this, FF now take each of their size groupings and rank the stocks in them by beta in each of the years. For the largest stocks, the 10% with the largest betas are placed in group 1a, the next 10% in group 1b, and so on. Then the monthly returns for each of the subgroups are observed from 1941 to 1990, and beta is plotted against average return. If beta were the true driving factor behind the return differentials of Figure 8-3A, the subgroups should fill in the gaps between the large stock grouping to the lower left and the smaller stock groupings to the upper right.

As we can clearly see in Figure 8-3B, they don't. The subgroupings appear as triangles and squares. Within the largest stocks, those with highest risk tend to have the lowest returns. The line of best fit passing through the subgroup scatter has a negative slope.[9] The same is true for the smallest stocks (the unshaded squares).

High risk, low return.

What the textbooks tout as a risk effect is really a liquidity effect.

"V"

Investors do not expect risky stocks to produce lower returns. The low returns come as a surprise. Much is expected of these expensive stocks in terms of future profitability.

Too much.

Mean reversion takes effect, and the actual performance is disappointing. As expectations are revised, returns on the risky, expensive stocks systematically turn out to be lower than expected.

High risk, low return.

If overreaction is behind the upside-down relationship between risk and return, we should see the relationship flip from right side up to upside down *when the market initiates its tendency to overreact.*

As discussed in Chapter 3, the market had a relatively brief flirtation with growth stock investing in the late 1920s. During the 1930s, 1940s, and through most of the 1950s, investing on the basis of projected growth was out of favor; instead, the prevailing investment philosophy was that espoused by Graham and Dodd in their book *Security Analysis*.[10]

In the early 1960s, growth stock investing made a comeback. Investing on the basis of projected future growth was once again accepted practice and would remain as such *until this day.*

This gives us two interesting and distinguishable time periods. Expensive, growth stock investing has dominated over the past 35 years. The views of Graham and Dodd dominated over the 30-year period prior to that.

If this is true, we should be able to see the risk–return relationship flip upside down, following the comeback of growth stocks. The relationship between risk and return should be primarily positive during the first period and primarily negative during the second.

To see if this is the case, we shall examine the cumulative difference in performance between a low-volatility portfolio and the S&P 500 stock index.

To build a low-volatility portfolio, we begin with stocks that are traded on the New York Stock Exchange. We start the experiment all the way back in January 1928. At the beginning of the first quarter of 1928, we find the combination of stocks (names and fractions of our money invested in each name) that would have produced the lowest possible volatility of return over the trailing 24 months (1926–27).

To ensure that low volatility *in the past* will be roughly consistent with low volatility *in the future*, we need to keep our portfolio diversified. That is, we need to avoid plunging too deeply into any one stock or any one industry. We also want to keep the composition of the portfolio relatively stable over time to avoid severe distortion of our results, as returns get eaten up by trading costs.

At the beginning of each quarter, we'll use Harry's Tool to find the portfolio with lowest possible *trailing* volatility,[11] subject to the following constraints:

1. No more than 5% of the portfolio can be invested in any one stock. The minimum is 0%. (Short selling is not permitted.)
2. No more than 20% of the portfolio can be invested in any one industry.
3. We can't invest in a stock more than three times its percentage of the market's total value. (If IBM constitutes 1.5% of the total market value of all NYSE stocks, we can't invest more than 4.5% of the portfolio in IBM.)
4. Turnover in the portfolio is constrained to 20%.[12]

We'll buy and hold the portfolio we build until April 1928. At the beginning of this next quarter, we'll once again build the portfolio that would have had the lowest volatility over the trailing 24 months using all constraints discussed above.

We continue doing this, quarter after quarter, until we reach the last quarter of 1992.

Then we'll see how our performance would have looked in the periods following portfolio construction.

If overreaction is behind what we see in the data, we should observe a V-shaped pattern in the cumulative difference in performance.

In the era of Graham and Dodd, expectations should be realized, on average. Risky stocks should produce higher returns. Low-risk stocks should produce lower returns. The low-volatility portfolio should tend to underperform the market average.

The cumulative difference in performance between the low-volatility portfolio and the S&P should initially trend downward.

After the renaissance of growth stock investing, overreaction sets in. Expectations become biased. Growth stocks produce lower returns than expected. Low-volatility value stocks produce higher returns than expected.

The cumulative difference in performance should trend upward following the renaissance of growth stock investing.

Down, then up. We should look for a V shape in the historical record of relative performance.

Let's see if we can find it.

The low-volatility portfolio will be constructed, at the beginning of each quarter, in accord with the diversification constraints discussed previously. At the beginning of each quarter, we will find the combination of all stocks listed on the New York Stock Exchange that would have had the lowest possible volatility over the trailing 24 months. We will hold this portfolio for the next quarter and then revise the weights according to the constraints.

Because we need two trailing years to compute the low-volatility portfolio weights, we can begin the experiment in 1928—two years after the beginning of the CRISP[13] tapes.

The cumulative difference between the return on the low-volatility portfolio and the S&P between 1928 and 1996 is plotted in Figure 8-4.

There it is!

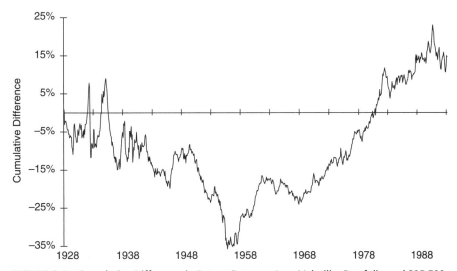

FIGURE 8-4 Cumulative Difference in Return Between Low-Volatility Portfolio and S&P 500

Down during the era of Graham and Dodd. Up during the modern age of growth stock investing.

And the V points to *the time of the renaissance!*

DOES RISK STILL CARRY A NEGATIVE PAYOFF?

The negative payoffs to risk documented above flies directly in the face of the cornerstone of Modern Finance. Let's update these results to see if it continues to be true.

According to The Theory, market beta should be the only factor distinguishing the expected returns from stock to stock. The larger the market beta is, the higher expected return should be.

Since stocks with higher betas are supposed to have higher *expected* returns, they should tend to have higher *realized* returns over long periods of time, as these expectations are realized. High beta stocks should tend to outperform low beta stocks.

Not always. But if they don't cover the ups and downs of the complete market cycle, we should seriously doubt if they will in the general case.

Let's see how they performed since the year 1990. We'll start in the first month of 1990. Taking roughly the largest 3,500 stocks in the U.S. market, we rank the stocks by their market betas, calculated over the trailing 36 to 60 months, depending on data availability. In each case, we relate the individual stock's returns to the returns to the S&P 500 stock index to obtain a measure of the stock's sensitivity to the returns to the index.

Then we rank the stocks by their beta sensitivity and form the stocks into equally weighted deciles. *Decile 10* will have the *highest* betas and *decile 1* the *lowest*. We will hold the deciles for a month and observe their returns. At the end of the month, we recompute the betas for each stock, again over the trailing 36- to 60-month period. The deciles are reformed and returns once again observed.

Do the high beta deciles produce higher returns?

Over the period of January 1990 through April 2008, the answer seems to be no!

But let's look at one of the years where the answer is yes. Figure 8-5A plots, for the year 1991, total annualized return against decile ranking. The line in the figure is the line of best fit. This line has a slope of 6.32%. That means if you move from a relatively low beta decile to the next higher decile, realized return can be expected to *increase* by 632 basis points.

Note how large the decile returns are on average. This was a bull market where all boats were rising. In this environment, it's not at all surprising that the deciles with stocks most sensitive to movements in the market did the best.

Figure 8-5B shows the results in a bear market. Here, as we would expect, the deciles with stocks with the *lowest* market sensitivities do the best.

So we expect the slopes to be positive in bull markets and negative in bear markets, but, in recent years, what has typically been the payoff to risk?

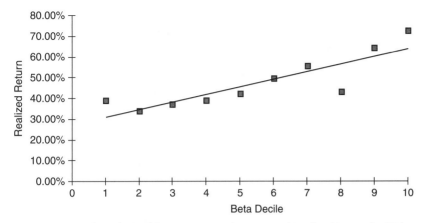

FIGURE 8-5A   The Relationship Between Market Beta and Realized Return in 1991

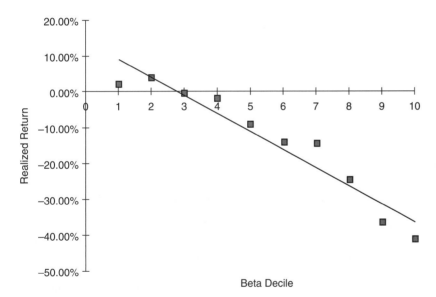

FIGURE 8-5B   The Relationship Between Market Beta and Realized Return in 2002

The slopes on a year-by-year basis, between 1990 through April 2008, are shown in Table 8-1. Note that the slopes are negative in 14 of the 20 years.

Once again, The Theory is struck down by the evidence.

Once again, we see mostly a negative relationship between risk and return, with the high beta deciles producing the lower returns.

Yes.

Be leery of The Theory.

TABLE 8-1 Slopes Associated with the Yearly Relationship Between Market Beta and Realized Return (January 1990 through April 2008)

Year	Slope
1990	−.03
1991	3.62
1992	−.10
1993	−1.72
1994	−.09
1995	2.13
1996	−.50
1997	−1.15
1998	.42
1999	6.26
2000	−2.25
2001	−.81
2002	−5.06
2003	8.70
2004	−2.65
2005	−.71
2006	.04
2007	−.23

APPENDIX: THE NEGLECTED HORIZON PROBLEM

Fama and French (FF) observe the relationship between risk and the simple average of the monthly rates of return to their stock portfolios. This procedure is unbiased if the horizon of investors is of one-month duration. *If the horizon of investors is longer than this, however, the slope estimates of FF are upward biased.*

Know that, if volatility is nonzero, the simple average of a time series of returns is always greater than the geometric mean, and the difference increases proportionately with the volatility.

Consider the following example. Two portfolios and two periods. Both portfolios are worth $100 at the beginning of the first and at the end of the second period. However, in the interim, Portfolio 1 falls to $50 and Portfolio 2 falls to $25, then they both rise back to $100. What is the simple average of their one-period returns? For Portfolio 1 it is 25% (−50% + 100%)/2. For Portfolio 2, the more volatile, it is 112.5% (−75% + 300%)/2.

The numbers 25% and 112.5% are unbiased estimates if the true horizon is one-period long. However, they are upward biased if the true horizon is two periods, and the bias is greater for the more volatile portfolio.

Thus, if the true horizon is something like five years, and we assume instead that it is a month, we will find a positive relationship between volatility (and most likely beta) and the mean of monthly returns even if there is no relationship between portfolio volatility and the true expected return over five years.

To see the extent of the bias, we'll perform the following experiment:

Assume that investors have a *five-year horizon.* Also assume that they don't care about risk, so over the five-year period all stocks have the same expected rate of return. *Now* pull, at random, 20, five-year (spanning a 100-year period) "portfolio" returns from a probability distribution with a 12.5% annual expected return and a 20% annual volatility. Next compute the arithmetic mean of the 20 five-year returns as well as their sampled volatility. Plot this first portfolio as one of the points in Figure A8-A.

Now repeat the process 199 times for 200 portfolios in all, each having a 12.5% expected return but different volatilities,[14] and plot each simulated portfolio as a point in Figure A8-A.

Note that there is no significant relationship between risk and realized, cumulative five-year return.

Now *we'll do what nearly everyone has done.*

This time we'll compute the mean of the 1,200 monthly rates of return for each portfolio and plot them against their monthly volatilities in Figure A8-B.

Ahah!

Now we find a positive relationship.

And it's highly significant with a coefficient of determination of 28.94% with a *T*-value for the slope of 8.98.

That's one of the best results for the cross section of risk and return ever found!

And we found it in a market in which investors don't care about risk.

But there are no risk premiums in our assumed market.

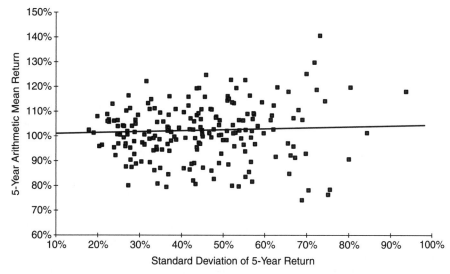

FIGURE A8-A Five-Year Arithmetic Mean Return versus Five-Year Standard Deviation for 200 Stocks with Equal Five-Year Expected Returns but Differential Standard Deviations

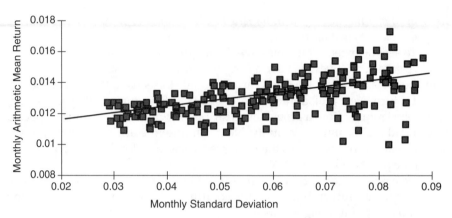

FIGURE A8-B   Monthly Arithmetic Mean Return versus Monthly Standard Deviation for 200 Stocks with Equal Five-Year Expected Returns but Differential Standard Deviations

However, we find what looks like evidence supporting the existence of risk premiums if we assume that the investment horizon is shorter than what it truly is.

FF provide no support for their assumed one-month horizon period. We don't really know the length of the true horizon, but I would find it easier to support the assumption of five years over one month. Quarters, as opposed to months, are the basic unit for measuring returns in the investment business. Five years is the typical interval for reconsideration of major asset allocation decisions by pension funds. Five years is also an important period for the analysis of the performance of investment managers. Most funds will not tolerate underperformance across a full five-year period. Moreover, a period of five years spans a typical cycle in business conditions.[15]

Notes

1. The graphs are taken from Table I, panels A and B of E. Fama and K. French, "The Cross-Section of Expected Stock Returns," *Journal of Finance* 47, no. 2 (June 1992).

2. Lines are plotted that will minimize the sum of the squared vertical distances of the ten observations from the line.

3. A. Ang, R. Hodrick, Y. Zing, and X. Zhang, "The Cross-section of Volatility and Expected Returns," *Journal of Finance* (2006).

4. Lettau and Wachter attempt to explain "how value stocks can have both higher returns and lower betas than growth stocks." See M. Lettau and J. Wachter, "Why is Long-Horizon Equity Less Risky? A Duration Based Explanation for the Value Premium," *Journal of Finance* (2007). They feel that they can explain this apparent contradiction if they assume that investors do not fear changes in the risk premium associated with stock investments. However, as we shall show in Chapter 11, the single most important determinant of variations in the daily rate of return to the S&P 500 are daily changes in the market's assessment of its volatility. As the level of volatility rises, the price level of the S&P falls, indicating a high level of risk aversion related to this volatility.

5. See also K. R. French, G. W. Schwert, and R. Stambaugh, "Expected Stock Return and

Volatility," *Journal of Financial Economics* (1987), pp. 3–29. Also R. A. Haugen, E. Talmor, and W. Torous, "The Effect of Volatility Changes on the Level of Stock Prices and Subsequent Expected Returns," *Journal of Finance* (1991).

6. It has been argued (See R. Roll and S. Ross, "On the Cross-Sectional Relation Between Expected Returns and Betas," *Journal of Finance* (1992) that the cross-sectional results are merely the result of selecting an index that is not the true market portfolio. However, the betas computed with respect to this index do represent the contribution that the individual stocks make to the volatility of the index. Because other studies clearly show that investors react negatively to unexpected increases in the volatility of the U.S. stock index, how can it also be that the same investors who fear volatility in the index expect the lowest rates of return from the stocks that make the greatest contribution to that volatility? The answer seems to be that they do not *expect* the relatively low returns. They come as a *surprise*.

7. *The Inefficient Stock Market What Pays Off and Why* (Upper Saddle River, NJ: Prentice Hall, 1999) I present two alternative, and perhaps complementary, explanations for the negative relationship between risk and return. As we shall see shortly, risk and return inverted at the time the fiduciary came to power in the market (the early 1960s). Since then, the market has been dominated by people who invest other people's money—fiduciaries. Fiduciaries have job-related agency problems, and these problems may have turned risk and return upside down. First, the pros have redefined risk. They are deathly afraid of underperforming the market. Risk isn't how much a stock goes up and down from day to day (volatility). Rather, they see risk as mismatches in the moves of a stock and the moves of the market index (tracking error). If a stock portfolio pretty much matches the day-to-day returns to the S&P 500, it's not risky in their eyes. A not very volatile utility stock has just as much chance to mismatch the S&P as a high-flying tech stock. So they see no reason to discount the price of the tech stock, so that it will produce a premium return.

In fact, there is a second job-related problem that makes the risky tech stock relatively *attractive* to them.

People who analyze stocks for a living know that it's crucial that they make a compelling case for the stocks they bring before their investment committees. They are attracted to interesting and exciting stocks—for which they can create a great story—stocks that are in the news. These stocks have prices that rise and fall more quickly with changes in the news, making them more volatile. But the pros see them as being more intriguing and interesting rather than simply more risky. Rather than sell at discounted prices because of their relative risk, intriguing stocks may sell at premium prices because they are exciting. Their stodgy counterparts—companies making bottle caps or toilet paper, for example—are less volatile. Rather than sell at premium prices because they are relatively safe investments, these companies may actually sell at discounted prices because they are boring and difficult to generate professional interest in.

8. The portfolios are equally weighted across the stocks.

9. Size and beta are obviously highly correlated. This will cause a multicollinearity problem in all regressions where size and beta appear together, which will make it difficult to interpret the coefficients on each variable. In N. Jegadeesh, "Does Market Risk Really Explain the Size Effect?" *Journal of Financial and Quantitative Analysis* (September 1992), portfolios are constructed to minimize the collinearity between size and beta. In multiple regressions with both variables, Jegadeesh finds a significant size effect, but a negative (but nonsignificant) relationship between beta and realized monthly return over the period 1954–89. Jegadeesh uses the CRISP database for his analysis, which is free from survival bias.

10. B. Graham and D. Dodd, *Security Analysis* (New York: McGraw-Hill, 1934).

11. Volatility is defined as standard deviation of monthly return (calculated including dividends as well as capital gains). Using a numerical procedure, we are able to find an exact solution (given the weighting constraints) to the problem without having to invert the covariance matrix of returns.

12. After considering the effects of trading on costs and expected volatility, trades are made until marginal trading costs per unit of reduced volatility reach a level consistent with 20% annual turnover in the portfolio.

13. Center for Research in Security Prices (University of Chicago).

14. Ranging from 10% to 30% annualized.

15. For the very first evidence supporting the notion supporting the notion of a negative relationship between risk and expected return using a five-year time horizon see R. Haugen and J. Heins, "Risk and Return on Financial Assets: Some Old Wine in New Bottles," *Journal of Financial and Quantitative Analysis* (1975).

CHAPTER 9

The Holy Grail

RECAP

To see the big picture, let's bring together much of what we have learned so far.

A cheap value stock: a stock selling at a cheap price relative to cash flow, earnings, dividends, and book value, and for which earnings per share might be expected to grow at a slower than average rate in the future.

An expensive growth stock: a stock selling at an expensive price relative to current cash flow, earnings, dividends, and book value, and for which earnings per share might be expected to grow at a faster than average rate in the future.

Cheap and expensive stocks are priced as though they will distinguish themselves, in terms of their relative growth, for many years into the future.

The idea that relative growth can be forecasted for *long* periods into the future—growth stock investing—has been visited upon us twice in the twentieth century. Each time it came, *no* evidence was brought forth that long-term future growth was, in fact, forecastable. Growth stock investing just came, went, then came back and stuck around.

In fact, because value companies tend to reorganize and reinvent themselves or are taken over and forced to do just that, and because growth companies face hungry competitors eager to participate in profitable product markets, the bad and the good become the average much faster than the market realizes. (See Figures 5-1 through 5-6.)

In the very short run, good earnings reports tend to be followed by a few more. This is also true of bad reports. Based on the observed behavior of stock returns, the market seems to react slowly to the beginning of these chains. However, *as several links of the chains fall into place, the market price appears to overreact*, anticipating that the chain of future positive (negative) reports is apt to be a very long one. In reality, the *subsequent* links in the chain are equally likely to reflect above- or below-average earnings performance. For growth stocks, the *above-average* reports that may come along are *expected*, so no significant positive price responses accompany their receipt. On the other hand, the *below-average* reports are *unexpected*. Because they are unexpected, their receipt is accompanied by downward price adjustments. *As a class*, expensive stocks subsequently produce poor returns for the unfortunate investors who bought them at inflated prices.

The opposite is true for cheap stocks—positive surprises and good returns as the bad firms of the past quickly revert to the average (see Figures 3-1A and 3-1B).

Because the market initially underreacts and then overreacts, we see evidence of the presence of *inertia patterns in the short run* and *reversal patterns in the long run*. These patterns show up in studies that compute various measures of volatility of return, where return is alternatively computed over weeks, months, and then years (see Figures 3-3 and 3-4).

In all long-term races between cheap and expensive stocks, *cheapness wins* (see Figures 6-2 through 6-5B). We should expect this in the presence of overreactive market prices. However, it may also be that investors expect and require the higher returns on cheap stocks because they are believed to be relatively risky. Based on the evidence presented thus far, we choose to dismiss this alternative explanation for GO because (a) the "risk premium" seems *unbelievably large*[1] (see Figure 1-2), (b) cheap stocks have *lower market risk in a market that clearly fears volatility* (see Figure 1-3), and (c) the *peculiar time pattern in the receipt of GO* around earnings announcement days (see Figures 3-1A and 3-1B) and at the turn of the year (see Figure 7-1).

Because the low-risk, cheap stocks tend to produce high returns and the high-risk, expensive stocks tend to produce low returns, *the market's fear of risk is overridden by its overreaction to past earnings trends.* Investors may in fact want higher returns on the relatively risky expensive stocks. But the risky, expensive stocks are priced too high relative to their *true* prospects. Actual results systematically tend to fall short of expectations, and the risky expensive stocks, as a class, tend to produce lower-than-average returns. The opposite is true for low-risk cheap stocks (see Figures 8-1A through 8-1J).

The story, thus far, in a nutshell.

LOOKING DOWN THE ROADS TO DIAMOND HEAD AND DIAMOND BAR

So, what does the future look like for value and growth? Given the way these stocks are priced at the time I write this book, what can we expect as a return on these investments over the next 20 years?

You may remember from Chapter 5 that the "judge" gave me permission to recall an exhibit from the "hot shots" (Figure 5-6). I'm going to exercise that privilege now.

Let's bring back the Christmas Tree and collect all the presents!

Figure 5-6 showed the relative growth rates in earnings per share for stocks grouped on the basis of the ratio of earnings per share to market price per share. It showed that in the years *after* the ranking by this ratio, the group of stocks with the largest prices in relation to current earnings (expensive stocks) grew faster than average and the group of stocks with the lowest prices (cheap stocks) grew more slowly than average.

However, as we move ahead to two, three, four, and five years after the rankings, the high- and low-priced stocks revert to the average in the growth of their earnings.

Let's assume that Figure 5-6 is a fair and accurate representation of the extent to which relative growth reverts to the mean as you move into the future.

If this is the case, can we say that the market is pricing stocks fairly with respect to this mean-reverting process *now*?

We will construct a sample of stocks[2] as of mid-2008 using the criterion similar to that which Fuller, Huberts, and Levinson used. We then rank the stocks on the basis of earnings per share to market price per share. The median values for the 20% of the stocks with the smallest earnings/price ratio (growth) and the 20% with the largest earnings/price ratio (value) and the three groups in between are as follows:[3]

Group	Earnings/Price Ratio
Lowest E/P (expensive)	2.51%
Low E/P	4.59%
Median E/P	5.94%
High E/P	7.62%
Highest E/P (cheap)	12.49%

To keep the math simple, assume an average market price of $100 for each group. This gives us average current earnings per share of $2.51 for the expensive stocks and $12.49 for the value stocks.

Now we need a long-term, nominal growth rate *for an average stock* to which the expensive and cheap stocks will eventually mean revert.

The nominal growth rate is the sum of the expected rate of inflation and the real rate of growth in inflation adjusted dollars.

Since 1926, common stocks in the United States have produced an 8% real (inflation-adjusted) rate of return for investors. Over the last decade, an average stock pays approximately 52% of returns as dividends and retains 48% for future growth, leaving $48\% \times 8\% \approx 4\%$ for real growth.

Now we need an estimate of long-term expected inflation. We'll assume 3%.[4]

Thus, our estimate of 4% for real growth in stockholder earnings plus our estimate of 3% in long-term inflation bring us to an expected nominal growth for an average stock of 7%.[5]

So we interpret the growth numbers on the horizontal axis of Figure 5-6 as growth rates relative to 7%. Thus, in the first year, the earnings of the expensive growth stocks can be expected to grow at 7% + 8.6% = 15.6% and the cheap value stocks at 7% − 9.9% = −2.9%.

However, remember that the cheap stocks start at earnings of $12.49 versus $2.51 for the expensive stocks.

Assuming that the various quintiles will follow the respective patterns of the bars of Figure 5-6 in the years beyond 2008, we can expect to get the time series of future earnings per share shown in Figure 9-1.

Given the initial lead held by the cheap stocks (higher first-year earnings) and the mean-reverting tendency of earnings growth, *the expensive stocks will never catch up.*

To find out what this means to our rates of return as stockholders, we must convert these earnings numbers into dividend numbers.

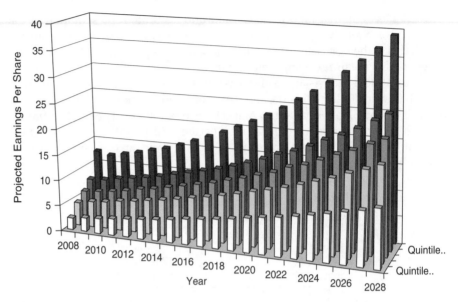

FIGURE 9-1 Projected Earnings per Share

So we calculate the average percentage of earnings paid out as dividends for each quintile. Assuming 52% as the percentage of earnings paid out as dividends, we can expect to get the time series of future dividends in Figure 9-2.

Again, the expensive growth stocks will never catch up.

Let's assume we sell the cheap and expensive stocks at mid-2028. At what price?

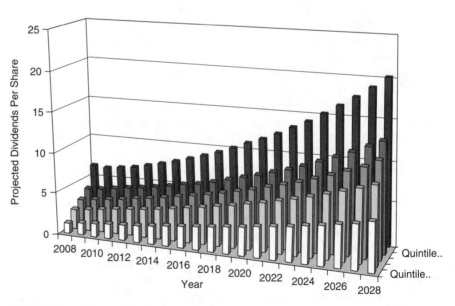

FIGURE 9-2 Projected Dividends per Share

Across all stocks in our sample, the median earnings multiple (the ratio of market price to earnings per share) at mid-2008 was 16.77. Assuming that the present is the best guess for the future and recognizing that both the cheap and expensive groups are likely to be viewed as average in 20 years, we apply this multiple to the 2028 values for earnings for the cheap and expensive groups, getting:

2023	Cheap:	$16.77 \times \$39.08 = \$655$
2023	Low:	$16.77 \times \$26.07 = \$437$
2023	Median:	$16.77 \times \$22.32 = \$374$
2023	High:	$16.77 \times \$18.41 = \$309$
2023	Expensive:	$16.77 \times \$11.43 = \$192$

With bigger expected dividends and a higher expected selling price for the stocks in the cheap group, we must expect a higher future rate of return. We can calculate the expected future internal rate of return based on the future selling price, the dividends, and the current price of $100 for each group.

The results for expected future return to:

Cheap:	15.86%
Low:	11.79%
Median:	10.42%
High:	8.90%
Expensive:	5.58%

True, these differences aren't as large as the historical (1963–90) differences found by Fama and French (FF) (Figure 1-1) but remember that FF looked at 10% groupings rather than the 20% groupings used here. In addition, the initial FF study has been criticized for survival bias.

In fact, the forward-looking gap between cheap and expensive has actually widened since the last edition of this book!

GO is bigger than ever!

From this simple exercise, we learn that *the relative pricing structure that was in place to produce the premium returns to cheap versus expensive historically is still in place in 2008 to produce similar relative returns thereafter.*

THE RELATIVE POSITION OF THE PERCEIVED AND TRUE GROWTH HORIZONS

Overall, the exercise of the previous section brings us to a simple but critical point:

Unless it reflects the presence of an enormous risk premium, the spread in today's earnings/price ratios between cheap and expensive (12.49% versus 2.51%) is too large, given the strong tendency for earnings growth rates to mean revert.

The wide spread in earnings/price ratios reflected the market's mistaken *perception* that investors can forecast relative growth rates in earnings for long periods into the future.

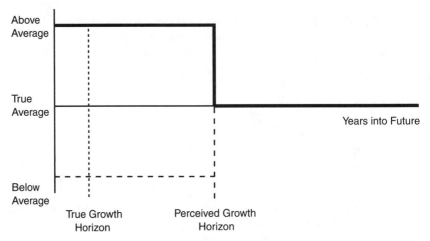

FIGURE 9-3A Overestimation of Short Run

In Figure 9-3A, we plot time into the future on the horizontal axis and growth in earnings, relative to the average, on the vertical. The market-expected growth rate of a stock perceived to initially grow faster than average is represented by the solid line above the horizontal axis. For simplicity, we have assumed that the mean reversion takes place *suddenly,* at the end of the growth horizon, rather than *gradually,* as it actually does in Figure 5-6.

A cheap value stock, expected to grow more slowly than average, is represented by the broken line of Figure 9-3A. It is also expected to mean revert suddenly, at the same time in the future as the expensive growth stock.

Call the number of years until the expected mean-reversion point the *perceived growth horizon.*

Note that, as the perceived horizon becomes longer, the relative market value of expensive stocks becomes *larger* (faster than average growth for longer periods into the future) whereas the relative market value of cheap stocks becomes *smaller* (slower than average growth for an even longer period of time). Given current earnings and expected growth differentials, the longer the perceived growth horizon, the wider the spread in earnings/price ratios between cheap and expensive ends of the spectrum of stock prices.

The vertical dotted line in Figure 9-3A represents the length of time we can *actually* forecast relative growth into the future.

Call the number of years until the true mean-reversion point the *true growth horizon.*

In looking at Figure 5-6 and recalling the results of I. M. D. Little and others, we can safely say that the true growth horizon is relatively short. In the context of an assumed sudden shift as opposed to gradual decline, perhaps it is only one or two years out.

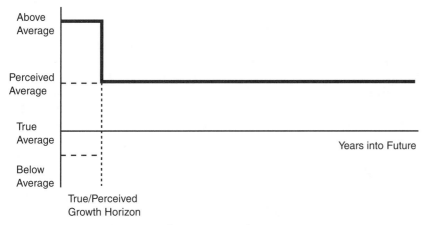

FIGURE 9-3B   Overestimation of Average Growth

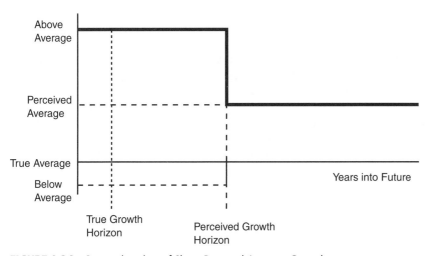

FIGURE 9-3C   Overestimation of Short Run and Average Growth

The market of Figure 9-3B has gotten the length of the growth horizon right; however, it has overestimated the *growth rate* of an average stock. The market of Figure 9-3C has an exaggerated view of both the average growth rate as well as the length of the growth horizon.[6]

In these contexts, cheap stocks have higher future expected returns for four possible reasons:

1. As in Figure 9-3A, the market is irrational and inefficient, and the perceived growth horizon is much longer than the true growth horizon. Competition will force mean reversion in relative growth rates much faster than the market expects. Today's investors will be *surprised* at the differential in return between today's cheap and expensive stocks when it is received.[7]
2. The market is irrational and inefficient, and the perceived and true growth horizons are of equal length. However, traders are systematically

overoptimistic about the average rate of growth, as in Figure 3-9B. According to supporters of this view, this error allegedly has more dire implications for the expensive stocks.[8] Today's investors will also be surprised at the relative performance.

3. Some combination of reasons 1 and 2, as in Figure 9-3C.
4. The market is rational and efficient, and (accepting the results of Chapter 4) the perceived growth horizon is relatively short and, in fact, equal to the true. Today's investors are aware of the true length of the short run and the differential in the future expected returns to value and growth stocks. They believe value stocks are more risky, and they require the differential as a risk premium. (This is the view of the Zealots.)

The "old timers" of the Ancient Finance had a perceived growth horizon of zero years. They didn't believe in taking future growth into account *at all*. This point of view was probably too extreme. Growth seems to be forecastable, if only for a rather short period into the future. On the other hand, the "hot shots" of the Ancient Finance and the expensive growth stock investors of today may have a perceived growth horizon as represented in Figure 9-3A or 9-3C.

There is now more direct evidence that reason 1 or possibly 3 may well be the best explanation for the relative performance of cheap and expensive stocks.

First, we have a study by Dechow and Sloan (DS),[9] who once again rank stocks traded on the NYSE or AMEX by the book-to-market ratio and then form into deciles. Their study spans the period from 1967 through 1991. For each firm in each year, they slide a line of best fit through the logarithm of the six most recently reported annual earnings-per-share numbers.[10] Taking the slope of the line as the past earnings growth, they find the average (across firms and years) past rate of growth for each book-to-price decile.

As is obvious from Figure 9-4, the extremely expensive stock deciles had much higher past rates of growth than did the extremely cheap stock deciles.

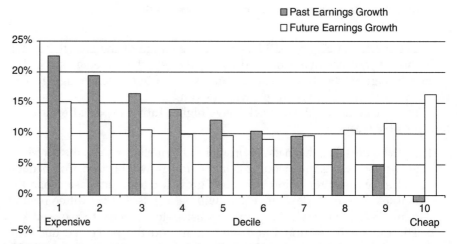

FIGURE 9-4 Past and Future Growth for Cheap and Expensive Stocks

Now DS look at the deciles' future five-year rate of growth (also plotted in Figure 9-4), measured in exactly the same way as was the past five-year rate of growth.

Mean reversion.

The expensive stocks tend to grow more slowly in the future than they did in the past and the cheap stocks tend to grow faster.[11]

If investors tend to extrapolate from the past into the future, they would be disappointed with the growth of the expensive stocks and pleasantly surprised by the performance of the cheap stocks.

A more recent study by Doukas, Kim, and Pantzalis[12] (DKP) provides a temporary "bump" in the road to a clear interpretation of the overall evidence.

DKP look at 44,536 earnings surprises over the period 1976 through 1997. An earnings surprise is defined as the median difference between an analyst's forecast for one year ahead (where each forecast is divided by the current market price of the stock) and the actual reported earnings for that year. Stocks are sorted into quintiles based on either their book-to-market ratios or their total market capitalization at the beginning of the year in which the forecasts are made.

Figure 9-5A shows the median forecast errors when sorted by size. Note first that the median errors are positive for all size groupings. The analysts tend to *overestimate* earnings. Note also that the degree of overestimation is nearly *20* times greater for the small stocks than it is for the large.

Later, we will provide a rationale for this pattern.

Figure 9-5B shows the results when the stocks are sorted by book-to-market ratio. Surprisingly, the analysts overshoot for the value stocks more than for the growth stocks. The errors are nearly five times greater for value than they are for growth!

This seems to fly in the face of all the evidence provided thus far. If investors expect too much from the growth stocks, why are the forecast errors smaller?

It's true that the market prices for the growth stocks are much bigger, and DKP scale by these prices, reducing the forecast errors for these stocks by

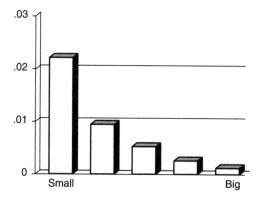

FIGURE 9-5A   Median Forecast Errors Sorted by Size Quintiles

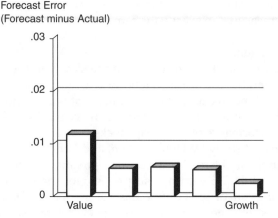

Forecast Error
(Forecast minus Actual)

FIGURE 9-5B   Median Forecast Errors Sorted by
Book-To-Market Quintiles

much more. However, DKP report similar results using earnings deflators like sales and assets, so we'll have to look for some other explanation.

As we shall see, the explanation lies in the pattern of overestimation overall and *much* greater overestimation for the small firms.

Before we explain, let's lay some more foundation.

First, a study by La Porta gives us *more direct* evidence that reasons 1 or 3 mentioned previously are closest to being on the money.[13] La Porta studies the earnings forecasts of professional analysts as surveyed by the Institutional Brokers Estimates System (IBES). The IBES numbers are watched *intensely* by investors. Thus, they have a very high status relative to ordinary survey data.

The study spans the period from 1982 through 1991 and covers an average of 900 firms per year traded on the NYSE and the AMEX.

For each company, La Porta looks at the change in the consensus estimate of earnings per share for a given year in going from the previous year to the year itself. That is, suppose the consensus estimate for a stock's earnings for 1991 was $1.00 in April 1990. A year passes. In April 1991, the consensus estimate for full-year earnings in 1991 is $1.10. The change is recorded as +0.10 dollars. Expectations are better *for* 1991 *in* 1991 than they were *in* 1990.

If the true growth horizon is indeed shorter than the perceived (Figure 9-3A), as we move forward in time, investors should be systematically disappointed by what they're discovering about the expensive stocks and pleasantly surprised about what they're discovering about the cheap stocks. Earnings estimates will be revised downward for the expensive stocks and upward for the cheap stocks.

If the true horizon is shorter *and* if investors are overly optimistic about the average growth rate (Figure 9-3C), then the downward revisions may carry into the cheap stocks, but the absolute magnitude of the revisions should diminish as we go from expensive to cheap.

La Porta ranks his stocks on the basis of consensus-expected growth in earnings per share in December of year –1 and forms them into deciles. Then, in April of year 0, he scales the consensus estimate of expected earnings in year +1 by the

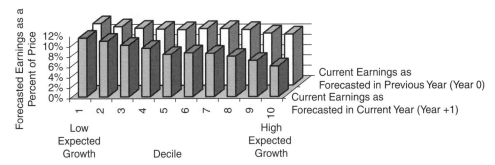

FIGURE 9-6 Earnings Estimate Revisions by Expected Growth Decile *Source*: R. La Porta, "Expectations and Cross-Section of Stock Returns," *Journal of Finance* 51, no. 5 (December 1996), p. 1730, Table IV.

stock price in April of year 0. He then compares this scaled estimate to the estimate made in April of year +1 scaled again by the stock price in April of year 0.

The back row of Figure 9-6 shows the average consensus estimates made in year 0 by growth decile. The front row shows the estimates made in year +1.

Aha!

All the estimates are being revised downward, but the revisions become smaller as we go from growth to value.

And now here's a really bone-crushing, "T-Rex" type fossil to show the Zealots.

Consider now a study of stock market reactions to earnings reports by La Porta, Lakonishok, Shleifer, and Vishny (LLSV).[14] Their study spans the period from 1971 through 1992 and covers a comprehensive list of firms on the NYSE, AMEX, and NASDAQ. As with many of the other studies covered in this book, stocks are ranked at mid-year by the ratio of book to market and deciles are formed. LLSV focus on the size-adjusted returns to the stocks in the deciles during the three-day window surrounding the announcements of earnings during the five years following decile formation.[15]

Figure 9-7 shows their results. We focus on the averages of the extreme deciles (1 and 2, and 9 and 10). The average size-adjusted price reactions to the

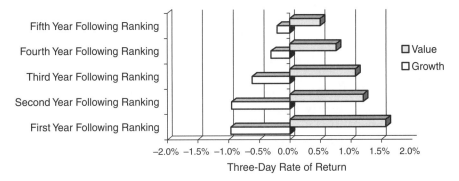

FIGURE 9-7 Returns of Growth and Value Stocks Around Earnings Announcement Dates

announcements (totaled across the four quarterly announcements each year) are shown in white for the expensive growth stocks and in gray for the inexpensive value stocks.[16]

On average, the announced earnings are clearly unpleasant surprises for the expensive stocks and pleasant surprises for the cheap stocks. And the differences are overwhelmingly statistically significant!

The Zealots are in a corner, and we are now are nearing the end of the line for The Fantasy.

Is it even *remotely* possible to think of the returns in Figure 9-7 as *risk premiums*? Remember, they cover only 12 days of the year—only 1/20 of the year's total number of trading days. The *annualized* size-adjusted return in the first year is 38% for the value stocks and –37% for the growth stocks. To attempt to call these mega-returns "risk premiums" quite simply *stretches the bounds of credibility to the point where continuing debate is of little interest to any but the most ardent of the Zealots!*

The evidence points to Figure 9-3A or possibly 9-3C, and reasons 1 or possibly 3, appear to be on the money.

The *clear* and *undeniable* case *against* reason 4 can be made on the basis of any or all of the following: (a) *the timing of the receipt of the so-called "risk premium" around earnings announcement dates and at the turn of the year,* (b) the relatively *low market risk of value stocks as documented by Fama and French,* (c) *the clear pattern of earnings estimate revisions in which the estimate of expensive stocks tend to be revised downward and cheap stocks upward, and finally* (d) *the clear difference in the nature of market reactions to earnings reports following the relative pricing of the cheap and expensive stocks.*

The proponents of The Fantasy stand precariously perched on their curious "risk-adjustment" evidence—in market environments during which value *doesn't* outperform growth and the difference between the returns to value and growth isn't statistically significant. (For the life of me, I still don't know why this self-fulfilling result is supposed to convince *anyone* of *anything.*)

One remaining puzzle piece must fall into place, however.

We still need to understand why DKP find that positive earnings surprises are greater for value than for growth stocks.

To fit this piece, remember two salient characteristics of their findings:

1. The median average earnings surprise is negative for all book-to-market and size groupings.
2. The absolute value of the median average earnings surprise is much greater for small stocks.

A recent study by Hong and Kubik[17] (HK) may help lock the DKP puzzle piece into place with the rest of the evidence.

You see, DKP aren't the only ones who find that analysts' earnings estimates tend to be overly optimistic. Brown, Foster, and Noreen (1985),[18] Dreman and Berry (1995),[19] and Chopra (1998)[20] all independently find that analysts' forecasts tend to overshoot. Moreover, Dechow, Hutton, and Sloan (1998),[21] Lin and McNichols (1998),[22] and Michaely and Womack (1999)[23] find that analysts from brokerage houses with an underwriting relationship with the stock being estimated overshoot even more.

It seems that the analysts are more concerned with their own job advancement than they are with accuracy. HK find that analysts who issue relatively optimistic forecasts are 90% more likely to move up the hierarchy in their firms. All this being the case, we can't take their forecasts as being unbiased estimates of their own expectations let alone that of the market.

The results of Figure 9-7 reflect the *market's* reaction to earnings surprises. Investors are clearly positively surprised by value and negatively by growth. How do we reconcile this with the results of Figure 9-5B?

Figure 9-8 shows us how.

The vertical axis plots expected growth in earnings per share. Book-to-market ratio is plotted on the horizontal axis. The true relationship between expected growth and book-to-market ratio is shown by the horizontal dotted line—. Growth stocks and value stocks are presumed in this figure to have the same true expected rates of growth. The analysts and the market have biased expectations, both believing that growth stocks will grow faster. Their expectations are depicted by the middle of the three broken lines.

We know value stocks are distinctly smaller companies. Growth stocks tend to be large, well-diversified companies. As such, uncertainty associated with their earnings estimates is likely to be much smaller than for the value stocks. The broken lines above and below the analysts' and market's expectations show growth rates that are one standard error above expectations.

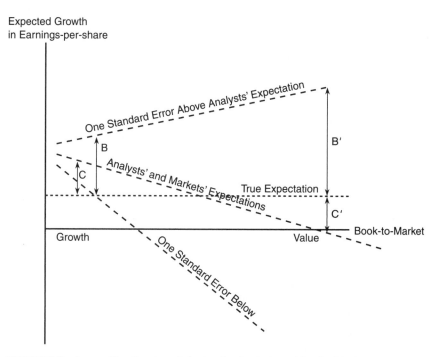

FIGURE 9-8 Reconciling Earnings Surprises by Analysts and by the Market

Suppose the analysts *are* more concerned by their desire for advancement than by accuracy. They know that advancement comes with optimism. Accordingly, assume they tend to issue estimates that are one-standard error above their expectations. This being the case, the "analysts' earnings surprises" for growth and value will be positive, but value will be greater as in line segments B and B'. Since value stocks are smaller, it will also be the case that the surprises for smaller stocks will be greater, as we saw in Figure 9-5A. At the same time the "market earnings surprises" will be negative for the growth stocks (line segment C) and positive for the value stocks (line segment C').

Last piece locked in.

BOTTOM FISHERS AND RODEO DRIVERS

Incidentally, there is another piece of anecdotal evidence that points to the conclusion that either reason 1 or 3 (above) is correct.

I think *they* know that investors tend to overestimate the length of the short run.

They are the managers of pension funds.

I think *they* know because they are willing to hire *many* money managers of a particular type, and they hire *none* of the opposite type.

The type of manager they hire is called a **Bottom Fisher**, one who sorts stocks on the basis of numbers that indicate cheapness in price. Bottom Fishers look for stocks with high ratios of earnings/price, dividend/price, book/market, and so on. They don't pretend to have a crystal ball. They don't consider the *future prospects* for a stock. They simply sort. They tout their disciplined approach to investing. They always buy and sell on the basis of their sorts.

Emotions never come into play.

Pension sponsors willingly hire Bottom Fishers, even though they know many of them are working without crystal balls.

But sponsors would never hire the *opposite* kind of manager.

These managers also invest without crystal balls. Don't consider prospects. Also sort. But these "Rodeo Drive"[24] managers go to the opposite side of the rankings. They look for stocks with *low* ratios of earnings/price, book/market, and so on. They look for the stocks that are *the most expensive,* and they buy them.

As a consultant, if I were to advise a sponsor to hire such a manager, you can count on the fact that I would be laughed at and summarily fired!

But such a manager would be expected to produce higher-than-average, risk-adjusted returns if the perceived growth horizon were actually **shorter** *than the true.* In such a world (pre–Edgar Lawrence Smith), the market would *underestimate the potential of growth stocks,* projecting above-average growth rates for a shorter period than justified given the true level of mean reversion. In this world, the growth stocks would be systematically underpriced and would subsequently produce superior returns for investors who bought them at bargain prices.

The Bottom Fishers can be expected to produce higher risk-adjusted returns, even without a crystal ball, only if the perceived horizon is *longer* than the true. *The fact that sponsors willingly hire Bottom Fishers and absolutely shun Rodeo Drivers implies that they sense that they are investing in an overreactive market.*

It seems that they realize that GO exists, but they don't reach for it.

Why?

Sponsors may be more concerned about keeping their jobs than they are about maximizing long-term retirement benefits.

They keep their jobs by matching the market, and this means hiring growth as well as value managers. (The growth managers are purportedly armed with better crystal balls to help them overcome the relative positions of the perceived and true growth horizons.)

As we learned in Chapter 6, growth stocks are big companies, and, as such, they dominate the market averages. Shunning growth in favor of value means investing in a portfolio that can't be counted on to move in tandem with the market. Although you increase your odds of outperforming the market averages in the long run, you increase the probability of significant underperformance in the short run.

"If I reach for GO, it may cost me my job!"

It is important to know that *they* know.

Because they are so powerful in the market, that, if they do reach for GO, it will disappear *for us.*

Without high levels of current wealth, we need the compounding effects of time to get to Diamond Head.

TWO COMPELLING QUESTIONS

The final case for GO requires answers to two compelling questions:

1. "Why hasn't all this been obvious before?"
2. "If the market is this inefficient, why do professional managers, as a group, consistently underperform the market averages?"

One reason this has escaped the attention of the investing public is the very short time horizons of the important players in the investment business. Pension sponsors pay very close attention to the performance of their managers. They are aided in this respect by the professional consulting industry. The standard of the consulting industry is to measure the performance of money managers over three trailing periods of time—the past year, the past three years, and the past five years.

Performance beyond the past five years is considered irrelevant because personnel and procedures employed by the money management firm in question have undoubtedly changed materially since then.

The studies that we have addressed in this book have been much longer term in nature. And it is only over the long term that the payoff to cheapness becomes so obvious.

But there is another reason that may be even more important.

Consider the relative stability of the true and perceived growth horizons of Figure 9-3A or 9-3C. The true horizon reflects the way the world actually is. This probably doesn't change very much over time. It is short because of the forces of competition and the propensity of below average firms to reorganize and reinvent themselves. Growth is relatively unpredictable now, and it has probably been that way for a long, long time.

We can't say the same about the *perceived* horizon, however.

We will go through periods in which, by chance, the market will experience an unusually low number of earnings surprises. This result may strengthen the market's confidence in its ability to forecast relative growth. Following these periods, stock prices may be restructured in a manner consistent with an *extension of the perceived growth horizon.* During these periods, the relative prices of growth stocks will go up. (Above-average growth will be expected for even longer periods into the future.) The relative prices of value stocks will fall (below-average growth will be expected for even longer periods). Expensive stocks will temporarily outperform cheap stocks, as they do from time to time. *Periods such as these will serve to reinforce the notion that growth stock investing may, infact, be a good idea.*

On the other hand, if we go through a period in which there is an extra-ordinary large number of earnings surprises, the market's confidence may be shaken and prices restructured in a manner consistent with a pulling back of the perceived growth horizon. In these times, the relative prices of stocks that were formerly cheap will climb dramatically (growth at below-average rates for shorter periods than previously expected).

As a result, GO does not come uniformly in time. In addition to its seasonal patterns (Figures 2-3A, 2-3B, and 7-1), *GO comes in "fits and starts" as the perceived growth horizon is extended and contracted.* Were it not for the instability in the perceived horizon, all of this would have been obvious a long time ago because it would have consistently shown up in the short-term monitoring of performances that continuously goes on in the pension industry.

GO shows up so clearly in the long-term studies assessed here because, *in the long term it makes no difference whether the perceived growth horizon is unstable.* What counts in the long term is the *average* relative position of the two horizons. If the perceived is extended beyond the true, the cumulative return to value investing will gradually (but not steadily) climb relative to growth investing. But, given sufficient instability in the perceived horizon, it won't be obvious except to those who are concerned with relative performance *in the long run.*

What about the second question? *Why do money managers as a group consistently underperform*? In the past, their underperformance has been a source of inspiration for the Zealots. After all, professional managers are supposedly better informed. Why should they underperform *unless* they are facing an efficient market in which all stocks are correctly priced? Their underperformance was supposed to stem from a wasting of money on the search for nonexisting stocks that aren't correctly priced.

The problem with the Zealots' explanation is that managers, as a group, are often underperforming by *more than they could reasonably be expected to be spending on analysis.* This is hard for the Zealots to explain, because in an efficient market, it is just as difficult to find an overvalued stock to buy as it is to find an undervalued stock.

But the professional money managers often seem to be turning the trick![25]

And why should they want to?

Why should they want to invest in overvalued stocks?

Unless overvalued stocks are good-looking stocks. Stocks with good records of success. Stocks with good press. Stocks doing well. Stocks that they can make a good case for in front of portfolio managers and investment committees. Stocks their clients will feel comfortable about having in their portfolios. Stocks that the market has overreacted to. Stocks that have risen in price too far. Stocks that will subsequently produce poor returns, *driving the performance of money managers as a group below the market averages.*

Why should they *not* want to invest in undervalued stocks?

Unless undervalued stocks are the ones with poor trailing records and bad press. Stocks their clients will feel uncomfortable about having in their portfolios. The ones with prices that have been driven down too far. The ones that will produce above-average returns in the future.

"Remove them from the portfolio so we won't have to explain to our clients why they're there."

The reason managers underperform is *not* because they are facing an *efficient* market.

Managers underperform because they have an agency problem with their clients, and, as a result, *they are the **victims** of market inefficiency!*

BAAAAAAAAAH HUMBUG!

Even after reading this book you may want to entrust your money to a manager who invests in expensive stocks.

You should be willing to do this, however, only if you believe that the manager has a really clear and powerful crystal ball and only if you believe he or she can find the expensive stocks with truly great prospects. You should also make sure that this manager carefully weighs the price to be paid for those prospects.

But you should be aware of one major concern.

If the institutional investors lose faith in expensive growth stock investing and engage in a massive restructuring of their portfolios, *the consequences will be tremendous.*

Looking ahead at the projected future returns to expensive and cheap stocks over the next 20 years, we see a wide gap between the growth and value extremes. If the institutional investors move to close that gap, woe to the investors in expensive growth stocks.

The expensive growth stocks must fall dramatically in price, and the cheap value stocks must rise dramatically.

If you invest in growth stocks, you face a possible loss of most of your wealth *if the institutions move.*

Will they move?

Probably not.

Why?

The fiduciaries are sheep, and the portfolios managed by the flock all look pretty much the same: some cash, a little real estate, a smattering of foreign stocks and bonds, a healthy chunk of domestic bonds, and a considerable commitment to domestic stocks. Most make a great effort (heartily endorsed by the professional consulting industry) to ensure that their stock investments are representative of the entire market—some growth stocks, some value stocks, and some small stocks.

Why? Because their benchmark is the S&P 500. The S&P represents 90% of the total value of the market.

And they don't want to be too different from their benchmark.

They don't want to act too differently from the other sheep.

They might stray from the flock and be eaten by the wolves that follow it.

They might underperform in the short run.

Let's take a closer look at the source of their fear. The source is a collection of laws called ERISA. Under it, fiduciaries can be sued and even face jail terms if they underperform and are found to have been *imprudent* in doing so. Corporate lawyers sit down with newly appointed pension officers and explain the perils of ERISA in clear and certain terms.

The pension officers then quickly appraise their position: They can lose, but they cannot win.

No one cares very much if they outperform the market. In fact, if they outperform by too much, they may be deemed guilty of taking unwarranted risk. They were imprudent but lucky. This time.

On the other hand, if they underperform, eyebrows are raised. Continuation of this pattern for three years means likely termination.

And *severe* underperformance can initiate real nightmares.

How can they keep from getting fired? How can they keep the nightmares from happening?

By looking as much like the "other guys" as they can. By building portfolios that look as much like their cap-weighted benchmarks (the S&P 500) as possible.

A tremendous amount of money would have to be moved to drop the prices of growth stocks. And given the real fears of the fiduciaries, it's unlikely that nearly that much will be moved, at their peril, away from their cherished benchmarks.

The individual investor doesn't have these hang-ups. When did you last worry about *S&P 500 tracking error* in your personal portfolio?

Haven't given it a thought, have you?

We can reach for GO with impunity. And we will. And those of us who do will bury the institutional investors with our relative performance.

The fiduciaries are now and will be afraid to reach for GO.

GO is for *us*.

Notes

1. The differential realized return between value and growth is approximately twice the realized differential between equities and T-bills. *Are we really to believe that investors perceive the risk differential between value and growth to be twice that of the differential between equities and T-bills?*

2. We eliminate stocks with negative earnings per share.

3. As with FHL, our groupings are industry diversified in accordance with their methodology.

4. At mid-2008, the rate of inflation in consumer prices was running at less than 3%.

5. The reader should note that this number is unimportant to the calculation of the *relative* expected future return on growth and value.

6. Nearly, all the evidence supporting this view should be discounted, since it is based on the earnings estimates of professional analysts. As we will see later on, analysts tend to overstate earnings for the good of their own professional advancement. In view of this, there is little support for the notion that these analysts actually tend to believe that earnings, in general, will be better than they actually turn out to be.

7. This was first discussed in R. Haugen, *Introductory Investment Theory* (Upper Saddle River, NJ: Prentice Hall, 1987), pp. 422–429.

8. P. Dechaow and R. Sloan take this view in "Returns to Contrarian Investment Strategies: Tests of Naïve Expectations Hypotheses," *Journal of Financial Economics* 43 (1997).

9. Ibid.

10. The slope of the line is the continuously compounded, annual rate of growth from one end of the line to the other.

11. They get very different results when ranking on measures of earnings to price, but this may be due to the fact that these measures perform less well as measures of cheapness. After all, the earnings yield may be low because (a) the price is high or (b) the earnings are low.

12. J. C. Doukas, F. Kim, and C. Pantzalis, "A Test of the Errors-in-Expectations Explanation of the Value/Glamour Stock returns Performance: Evidence form the Analysts' Forecasts," *Journal of Finance* (October 2002).

13. R. La Porta, "Expectations and the Cross-Section of Stock Returns," *Journal of Finance* (December 1996).

14. R. La Porta, J. Lakonishok, A. Shleifer, and R. Vishny, "Good News for Value Stocks: Further Evidence on Market Efficiency," *Journal of Finance* (June 1997).

15. This time, the window includes the day before the announcement in the *Wall Street Journal* the day of and the day after.

16. Firms are ranked into size deciles. For firms in the corresponding size decile that are neither growth nor value, the returns around *their* earnings announcement dates (in the same quarter) are subtracted from the returns to the firm in the value or growth group.

17. H. Hong and J. Kubik, "Analyzing the Analysts: Career Concerns and Biased Earnings Forecasts," *Journal of Finance* (February 2003).

18. L. Brown, G. Foster, and E. Noreen, "Security Analyst Multi-year Earnings Forecasts and the Capital Market" (paper presented at the annual meeting of the American Accounting Association, Sarasota, FL, 1985).

19. D. Dreman and M. Berry, "Analysts' Forecasting Errors and their Implications for Security Analysis," *Financial Analysts Journal* 51 (1995).

20. V. Chopra, "Why So Much Error in Analysts' Earnings Forecasts?" *Financial Analysts Journal* 54 (1998).

21. P Dechow, A. Hutton, and R. Sloan, "The Relation Between Analysts' Forecasts of Long-Term Earnings Growth and Stock Price Performance Following Equity Offerings" (working paper, University of Michigan, 1998).

22. H. Lin and M. McNichols, "Underwriting Relationships, Analysts' Earnings Forecasts, and Investment Recommendations," *Journal of Accounting and Economics* 25 (1998).

23. R. Michaely and K. Womack, "Conflict of Interest and Credibility of Underwriter Analyst Recommendations," *Review of Financial Studies* 12 (1999).

24. Because managers like this don't really exist, I had to invent their name based on the most expensive shopping area known anywhere.

25. See J. Lakonishok, A. Schleifer, and R. Vishny, "The Structure and Performance of the Money Management Industry," Brookings Papers: Macroeconomics, 1992.

CHAPTER 10

The Real Determinants of Expected Stock Returns

With Nardin Baker[1]

WHAT PAYS OFF IN THE STOCK MARKET

Throughout most of this book, we learned that cheap (value) stocks tend to have higher expected returns, that is, cheapness tends to have a positive payoff. We also learned that risky stocks tend to have lower expected returns, that is, risk tends to have a negative payoff. These assertions will be reinforced by the evidence presented in this chapter. However, we will also discover that there are other important determinants of expected return. For example, it turns out that stocks that are currently more profitable have higher expected returns. This seems to fly in the face of all the evidence we've seen on growth stocks, but it comes with a very important caveat—*given the price that you must pay for a stock,* it's simply better to buy stocks that are more profitable than less profitable. It also turns out that stocks that have done well in the last 12 months will tend to do well for a while. This is consistent with the inertia in the intermediate term that we discovered in Chapter 3. The most remarkable market behavior we will see is how incredibly *consistent* the pattern of payoffs is. What pays off in one decade pays off in decades to follow with the same sign and high degrees of statistical significance.

ESTIMATING PAYOFFS

Suppose that you are looking at the cross section of stock returns for the United States in a particular month. You want to determine whether cheap stocks tended to produce higher returns for the month. You select earnings-to-price as your measure of cheapness. Then you plot realized return for each stock during the month against the earnings-to-price ratio for each stock at the beginning of the month. Figure 10-1 shows a hypothetical example of such a plot, where each point is a single stock.

To estimate the payoff, we slide a line of best fit[2] through the scatter. The slope of this line (y/x) is the payoff to earnings-to-price. In this example, it's positive. Cheaper stocks *tend* to produce higher returns for the month.

FIGURE 10-1   Estimating the Payoff to Earnings-
to-Price

Suppose you want to *simultaneously* estimate the payoffs to (a) cheapness and (b) risk during the same month. As your measure of risk, you select the standard deviation (volatility) of the returns to each stock measured over the past 60 months. Let's stick to earnings-to-price as our measure of cheapness. This time *we plot all the stocks in three dimensions (as in Figure 10-2), where the month's return for each is plotted on the vertical scale, the earnings-to-price on one horizontal scale, and volatility on the other. Think of the graph as the corner of a room where returns are measured going up the corner toward the ceiling and earnings-to-price and volatility are measured on the floor along the two walls.

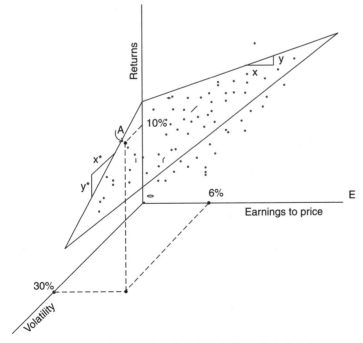

FIGURE 10-2   Simultaneously Estimating the Payoffs to Earnings-
to-Price and Volatility

TABLE 10-1 Calculating the Expected Return for Stock A

Projected Payoff to E/P	×	Beginning of Month E/P (Stock A)
+ Projected Payoff to Volatility	×	Trailing 60-month Volatility (Beginning of the Month) (Stock A)
	= Total Expected Return (Stock A)	

Now plot each stock as a point in the room. For example, the stock marked "A" is plotted at 10% off the floor and is positioned on the floor at a 6% earnings-to-price and at 30% volatility. Each of the other stocks is plotted similarly. We now slide a *plane* of best fit through the data. The slope of the plane (Y/X) going up the earnings-to-price wall is this month's payoff to this measure of cheapness. The slope of the plane (Y^*/X^*) going down the other wall is the payoff to volatility. In this month, the payoff to earnings-to-price is positive while the payoff to volatility is negative. We will see that this is generally true in real data.

If we repeat this exercise month after month, we can develop a history of the monthly payoffs. We can then use that history to make a projection of the payoffs for the next month. Our projection might be the simple average of the payoffs in the trailing 12 months. An estimate of expected return to each stock might then be obtained as in Table 10-1.

This process can be repeated for each of the stocks of Figure 10-2, obtaining an expected return for each stock. This method of computing expected return is called an expected return factor model. The factors in the model are things like earnings-to-price and volatility. You can simultaneously estimate the payoffs to three or more factors through a statistical process called multiple regression. You just can't visualize the multi-dimensional estimation process as we could with the two-dimensional Figure 10-1 or the three-dimensional 10.2.

AMAZING CONSISTENCY

Throughout this chapter, we will be looking at an expected return model that contains approximately 70 factors. These factors can be grouped into measures of (a) risk, (b) liquidity, (c) profitability, (d) cheapness, and (e) price history. In every month from January 1963 through December 2007, we use multiple regression to measure the payoff to each of the 70 factors over the roughly 3,000 largest stocks in the United States.[3] We then average the payoffs for each factor across all the months and compute a *T* statistic for each mean.[4] The larger the *T*, the more confident we can be that the average payoff is truly different from zero. With 60 monthly observations, a *T* of approximately ±2.00 indicates statistical significance with 95% confidence.

We then rank the factors by the absolute value of its *T* statistic. For the entire period (1963 through 2007), the 12 factors with the highest *T* scores are computed and presented in Table 10-1.

TABLE 10-2 *T*-statistics on the 15 Most Significant Factors

Period	1963–07	1963–72	1973–82	1983–92	1993–02	2003–07
$\in_{t-1}$	−22.4	−13.7	−15.9	−12.9	−7.2	−2.7
Cash-to-Price	13.9	6.4	12.7	8.6	4.3	4.1
Earnings-to-Price	13.1	4.0	11.4	8.3	5.3	1.9
Ret. on Assets	12.6	6.8	7.5	7.5	4.2	3.3
Residual Risk	−11.1	−3.5	−6.7	−8.8	−4.7	−1.9
12-month Return	10.8	5.0	5.7	6.9	5.1	1.1
Ret. on Equity	10.2	7.0	3.7	6.2	3.9	1.4
Volatility	−9.0	−2.3	−5.6	−7.1	−4.5	−2.0
Book-to-Price	8.9	2.0	6.2	6.7	3.2	3.1
Profit Margin	7.8	1.0	4.3	6.0	5.7	1.5
3-month Return	−7.2	−5.1	−6.9	−2.8	−.9	−1.5
Sales-to-Price	7.0	1.4	3.9	5.3	3.5	2.8

In each month from January 1963 through December 2007 the cross section of realized stock returns regresses on 70 characteristics (factors) of each stock using a weighted least squares procedure. The regression coefficients are averaged and *t*-statistics are computed. The *t*-statistics for the 15 most significant factors over the entire period are displayed in the first column. The *t*-statistics for the sub-periods are displayed in the other columns. The factor values are computed as:

- $\in_{t-1}$ is last month's residual stock return unexplained by market.
- Cash-to-Price is the 12-month trailing cash flow-per-share divided by the current price.
- Earnings-to-Price is the 12-month trailing earnings-per-share divided by the current price.
- Ret. on Assets is the 12-month trailing total income divided by total assets.
- Residual Risk is the 24-month trailing variance of residual stock return unexplained by market return.
- 12-month Return is the total return for the stock over the past 12 months.
- Ret. on Equity is the 12-month trailing earnings-per-share divided by the current book equity.
- Volatility is the 24-month trailing volatility of total stock return.
- Book-to-Price is the current book-to-price ratio.
- Profit Margin is earnings before interest divided by sales.
- 3-month Return is the total return for the stock over the past three months.
- Sales-to-Price is the 12-month trailing sales-per-share divided by current price.

The first column of Table 10-2 shows the *T* statistics for these factors for the entire period. Note first that the absolute magnitudes of the *T*s are quite large. The probabilities that these factors have non-zero values are all very close to 100%. Note also that the factors measuring cheapness in price (earnings-to-price, cash-to-price, book-to-price, and sales-to-price ratios) all have average payoffs that are positive. This means that, over the entire period, cheap stocks have tended to produce higher returns.[5]

Now note that the *T* statistics for all the measures of profitability—return on assets, return on equity, and profit margin—are all positive. This means that relatively profitable stocks have tended to produce higher returns. Why? Because the inefficient stock market prices stocks with imprecision—assigning different prices to stocks that are equally profitable and the same price to stocks with differing levels of current profitability. This means that *given the price you have to pay*, you're better-off buying stock in a company that is more profitable rather than less.

As expected, the factors representing risk (residual risk and variance of return) have negative *T* statistics, indicating that higher-risk stocks tend to have lower rates of return. Incidentally, market beta is well down on the list of factors of significance.

The *T* for one-year trailing total return is positive,[6] indicating momentum in the intermediate term.[7] We also see reversals in short-term returns (1 month and 3 months), indicating the market's tendency to correct overreactions to individual events.

PREDICTING THE FUTURE WITH MACHINES

The expected return factor model does an amazing job of explaining the cross-sectional differences in realized stock returns. One would think that the expected return factor model might be capable of predicting *future* returns on common stocks.

Let's see.

At the beginning of 1963, using information that was actually available at the time, we will go through a procedure akin to that presented in Table 10-1 (but with 70 factors instead of 2). That is, we will calculate the expected future return (for the first month of 1963) for each stock in our database. Then we will rank the stocks by their expected returns and form into deciles (10% groupings). Decile 10 will have the stocks with the highest expected returns and Decile 1 the lowest. During January 1963, we will observe what the stocks in each of the ten deciles actually produce. Then, at the beginning of February, we re-compute the expected returns, re-form the deciles, and observe the actual returns produced. At the end of 1963, we link[8] the 12 actual returns produced to form an actual total return for the year.

In Figure 10-3, we plot the relationship between decile ranking and the actual linked return produced by each decile in 1963. As you can see, the higher

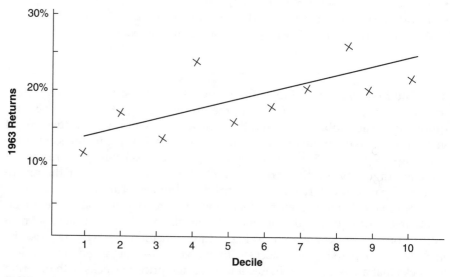

FIGURE 10-3   Decile Ranking versus Realized Return in 1963

TABLE 10-3 Spreads for Decile Lines of Best Fit for Each Year

1963	9.18%	1979	22.41%	1995	14.22%
1964	12.24%	1980	27.45%	1996	10.44%
1965	29.97%	1981	33.66%	1997	46.44%
1966	9.45%	1982	48.60%	1998	23.76%
1967	49.14%	1983	39.06%	1999	31.86%
1968	13.77%	1984	49.68%	2000	44.64%
1969	32.40%	1985	36.59%	2001	57.42%
1970	43.29%	1986	46.35%	2002	60.21%
1971	14.67%	1987	26.73%	2003	−5.49%
1972	29.70%	1988	18.54%	2004	21.06%
1973	44.37%	1989	32.22%	2005	12.78%
1974	30.69%	1990	33.39%	2006	7.47%
1975	30.87%	1991	27.72%	2007	29.07%
1976	32.40%	1992	10.62%		
1977	24.39%	1993	14.04%		
1978	7.83%	1994	16.83%		

the decile ranking, the higher the return tends to be. The positively sloped line is the line of best fit for the deciles. The spread from the bottom end of the line to the top is 9.18%.

This process is repeated for each year from 1963 through 2007. The spreads from the bottom to the top of the lines of best fit are shown in Table 10-3.

Obviously, the 70-factor model is extremely consistent in terms of the accuracy of its predictions. It should be stressed that there is a great deal of turnover in these deciles, especially in 10 and 1. Thus, after trading costs your returns will be lower. In fact Hanna and Ready[9] (HR) have shown that the spread between deciles 10 and 1 nearly disappears if trading costs are considered. However, it would be highly irrational to attempt to hold a Decile 10 portfolio. Many billions of dollars are actually invested on the basis of the 70-factor model. Real investors use the expected returns from the model in conjunction with some form of Harry's Tool to build portfolios that have low risk and very high returns. If you go to the Web site www.QuantitativeInvestment.com and enter the section on "Our Performance," you will see the results of investing equally in the highest 50 expected return stocks, while turning the portfolio over at an annual rate of approximately 100%. Given the population of stocks considered (the 1,000 largest), round-trip trading costs are likely to be under 1%. So simply subtract this amount from the annual return to see the returns on a net basis.[10]

HR contend that, since, based on their results, trading costs eliminate outperformance with the 70-factor model, the "risk premiums" reported in Table 10-2 don't have to be seriously considered. We do not understand this contention. The risk premiums reported in tests of the theoretical models of finance are pathetic in comparison to those of Table 10-2. Should we dismiss any support of the theoretical results because trading on the basis of the theoretical models fails to produce outperformance net of trading costs?

RISK PREMIUMS?

Advocates of the efficient market theory would argue that the superior returns of Decile 10 are merely rewards to risk-bearing.

However, Haugen and Baker[11] show that in moving from Decile 1 to Decile 10, there is a gradual and consistent transition in the character of the stocks in the deciles, and it's certainly not consistent with risk-bearing in Decile 10.

The stocks of the low-expected-return Decile 1 (a) are more volatile in their returns, (b) have higher market betas, (c) are smaller, (d) and are unprofitable and are in financial distress, and (e) their profitability is on the downtrend. On the other hand, the stocks of Decile 10 have lower volatility and lower market betas, they are larger, more liquid companies, and, in terms of profitability, they are good and getting better.

Once again we find that, in all dimensions of risk, the risky stocks are producing the lowest rates of return.

Notes

1. Nardin Baker is Chief Investment Officer for Quantitative Equity Management LLC, an institutional investment advisor that manages assets using factor-based analysis.
2. The line of best fit is the unique line that minimizes the sum of the squared vertical distances from the line.
3. In 1963, the sample consisted of 650 stocks. That number grew steadily until it reached 3,000 in 1973. From 1973 on, the sample consisted of the largest 3,000 U.S. stocks.
4. The T statistic is computed as (Mean Payoff)/(Standard Deviation) × (Square Root of N), where "Standard Deviation" is the standard deviation of the monthly payoffs and N is the number of monthly payoffs used to compute the mean.
5. This is true for all ten-year periods. However, as discussed in Chapter 9, there will be brief periods when expensive stocks outperform.
6. Note that the value of the T has shrunk considerably in the final four-year period. This is in part due to the small number of monthly observations used in computing the T. However, it may also be due to the large number of analysts who are

"playing" momentum in the stock market. They may be pricing this factor away.
7. Some have suggested that a model like this one should suffer from multicollinearity. They contend that correlation (within the cross section) between factors such as return on equity and return on assets should render the payoff estimates unstable. But how do they explain the extraordinarily high T statistics? Unstable payoffs would make the standard errors of the means high and the T statistics low.
8. To link the returns, add 1 to each and multiply as in $(1+r_1) \times (1+r_2) \times \ldots \times (1+r_{12})$. Then subtract 1.00 from the product. Then multiply by 100 to produce a percentage return.
9. J. D. Hanna and M. J. Ready, "Profitable Predictability in the Cross-section of Stock Returns," *Journal of Financial Economics* (2005), pp. 463–505.
10. If you wish, you may see audited reports of the performance of the 70-factor model as well as competing models. We, as well as our competitors, send our predictions of "buys," "holds," and "sells" at the beginning of each month to an auditor. The auditor keeps track of the results and publishes them

on the Web site www.investars.com. To see data on performance, enter "investors light" and select "compare analyst-to-analyst performance." Then rank the firms on some measure of performance. We are pleased to say that, as of the writing of this fourth edition, the 70-factor model is ranked number 1 for a trailing 2-year period.

11. R. Haugen and N. Baker, "Commonality in the Determinants of Expected Stock Returns," *Journal of Financial Economics* (1996), pp. 401–439. For an expanded version of this chapter, the reader is referred to R. Haugen and N. Baker, "Case Closed" (Handbook of Portfolio Construction; Contemporary Applications of Markowitz Techniques, 2009. "Case Closed" can also be downloaded at http://ssrn.com/abstract=1306523.

CHAPTER 11

Dangerous
Conversation

CONVENTIONAL WISDOM

On June 6, 2008, I paid a visit to the Museum of Communism in Prague, the capitol of the Czech Republic. A brass plaque at the entrance to the exhibits read as follows:

> The economic results of Czechoslovakia's industry reached their peak in the late spring of 1929. In the Fall the New York Stock Exchange collapsed and catalyzed an international economic crisis. The crisis had a decisive impact on Czechoslovakia in 1931 when exports were struck to the ground and the unemployment rate soared upwards. By 1933, one million citizens had been directly affected. The state could not avoid the rise of poverty and hunger and the communists took advantage of this via political and social agitation. The bordering regions were hardest hit where the 'consumption' industries continued losing the bulk of their market places. The suffering was felt most acutely by the German population which started to look up to Adolph Hitler. The Czechoslovakian crisis lasted for a long time and started to recede only in the second half of the thirties, thanks to the military contracts which strengthened the defense industry of the country. Hitler did not hide his intention to liquidate Czechoslovakia and to attach the Sudentland to the 3rd Reich.

Let's call the view presented on the plaque "conventional wisdom": The stock market in the United States collapsed, leading to the Great Depression that spread to Europe, which in turn led to the desperate economic conditions the Nazis took advantage of in their rise to power.

Advocates of Modern Finance would interpret these events in a different way. They would say that the collapse of the stock market did not, in any way, cause the Great Depression. Rather, they would contend that, in late 1929, events unfolded that enabled investors in the stock market to predict the onset of a great depression. The collapse of the market, they would argue, was simply a reaction to this correct prediction. They would argue that the stock market in no way acted as a causal influence.

In this chapter, we provide evidence and arguments in support of the conventional wisdom. We shall argue that:

a. The stock market is capable of collapsing at any time of its own accord.

b. Collapses in the stock market are typically associated with explosions in stock volatility. Risk-averse investors dramatically discount the current levels of stock prices because they want higher *future* returns during the period of market turbulence.

c. Should high volatility persist:

1. It increases uncertainty on the part of individuals and corporate investors, causing them to delay action on consumption and investment decisions.

2. It dramatically increases the cost associated with financing with equity capital, at least over the period over which the high volatility is expected to persist.

3. Individuals may further pull back on consumption as they experience wealth effects associated with the reduced value of their stock investments.

d. As turbulence in the stock market speaks to individuals and corporate investors, the resulting declines in consumption and investment spending speak back to the stock market, resulting in a conversation that can be both dangerous and destabilizing to the economy.

The most controversial of these arguments are (a) and (b). How can stock volatility explode of its own accord, resulting in a collapse in stock prices?

THE FINANCIAL CIRCUS

I'm sure you have seen the percentage changes in the S&P 500 stock index reported on the cable and network news. Given a series of these daily percentage changes, how would you measure its volatility? Technically speaking, volatility can be defined as the standard deviation of the series of returns or percentage changes over a trailing past period. The variance of the series is its standard deviation squared.

In *Beast on Wall Street*,[1] I divide stock volatility into three parts.

Event-driven volatility stems from instantaneous and unbiased changes in stock prices in response to information about real economic events. In the efficient market scenario, this would be the entire story. But the evidence in this book has revealed that stock prices tend to underreact to some types of information and overreact to most.

Error-driven volatility stems from these over- and underreactions and, ultimately, the corrections thereof. As we learned in the preceding chapters, the market overreacts to success and then corrects when it realizes that success is transitory. The overreaction and the correction add to volatility.

Over an interim period, the error-driven contribution can even be negative! The market underreacts to the first of a series of positive or negative earnings reports, and the reaction is delayed until the receipt of the following reports in the series.

Price-driven volatility is the final component. Given the evidence in *Beast*, it is the largest and most unstable component, and it stems mostly from market reactions to changes in the stock market's estimate of the underlying risk. Changes in its estimate of risk stem from the reaction of traders to previous and current trades and the resulting price changes in a given stock or in other pertinent stocks.

In *The Inefficient Stock Market*,[2] I provide an analogy that serves to more clearly define the three components.

You are at the Financial Circus watching a high-wire act. There are many aerialists on the wire, each holding a balance pole. Let the aerialists represent the market for individual stocks, and let movements in their balance poles represent movements in the stock price induced by trades. The wire is often shaken. Let these shocks to the wire represent impulses of information about real economic events.

The aerialists must respond to the shocks by adjusting their balance poles.

Think of the best and most efficient adjustments humanly possible. These are the movements associated with a completely efficient market; these are associated with event-driven volatility.

It turns out that the aerialists are not very good. They make mistakes with their balance poles, overreacting to some shocks to the wire and underreacting to others. These over- and underreactions and their subsequent corrections are analogous with error-driven volatility.

Afraid of falling, the aerialists begin watching each other for guidance. I adjust my balance pole in response to movements in yours, mostly unaware that *you* are also watching *me*. Our complex interactions create a dynamic that is unstable and, at times, dominates the movements in all balance poles. This is akin to price-driven stock volatility.

Now let's move from the aerialists to the real market.

In strictly efficient markets, prices rise and fall in instantaneous response to changes in the complete information set, presumed to be equally accessible to all market participants. In this strange world, speed in channels of information is infinite, and all market participants receive all increments of new information at precisely the same time. With infinite speed, everyone gets the information simultaneously.[3] It makes no difference whether you are upstream in a channel, positioned to receive information first, or downstream, positioned to receive it later.

In this strictly efficient market, stock prices react instantaneously to changes in the real information set. Here, stock price changes, themselves, are redundant to this set.

More generally, however, in the real stock market, information passes from investor to investor through potentially long and intersecting channels at finite and varying speeds. It is received sequentially, in accordance with an investor's position in a channel. Those positioned downstream are likely to look for behaviors signaling the receipt of a piece of event-related information upstream.

In this setting, institutional traders and brokers (agents) execute the trades of their principals (investors). The agents are loath to disclose even the identities and especially the positions of their principals in the channels of information.

In this context, real, event-related information received in the market for one stock will induce a price change that serves as a signal to investors downstream. Define trades that are induced by the receipt of real information as *higher-order trades*. Price changes induced by higher-order trades may induce subsequent trades, especially for the stock itself and also for others in the stock's peer group. Call trades that are induced by signals taken from price changes *lower-order trades*.

If you make the assumption that the reactions to price signals are *rational*, *orderly*, and *uniform*, lower-order trades may simply increase speed in channels of information. However, as shown clearly in this book, *price* reactions to *real events* are often irrational. Accordingly, market participants may not react in an orderly and unbiased fashion to the *signals* associated with changes in stock prices. If these reactions are not unbiased, lower-order price changes may provide fuel for still more lower-order changes. Note that an investor who is downstream for one impulse of information may be upstream for another. Thus, lower- and higher-order reactions may be confused, and lower-order reactions to the receipt of information about a real economic event may actually be occurring both up- and downstream.

The intensity and sequencing of *lower*-order trading may become the *focus* of many. This focus is not unwarranted, because the risk associated with price fluctuations stemming from erroneous lower-order trades is just as *real* as the risk associated with real economic events.

For example, if you log on to Yahoo Finance and discover that one of your investments is dropping like a rock, you are likely to make a hasty decision to buy, sell, or hold. Are you really responding to the event that triggered this slide or are you responding, at least in part, to the change in the value of your shares? I believe that to dismiss the possibility that investors respond to random changes in price that are unrelated to changes in the real information set is unrealistic at best.

Of course, higher- and lower-order trades stemming from *reactions* to real economic events and their associated price changes are not the whole story. Adding to the confusion, we have trades that are nonreactive. These "administrative" trades are associated with portfolio rebalancing, dividend reinvestment, the firing and hiring of investment managers, shifts in asset allocation, investor drawdowns and buildups to their portfolios, and routine repurchases of stock by corporations trying to avoid double taxation of dividends.

In the case of higher-order, lower-order, and administrative trades, what's observable, except by those associated with the trade, are (a) the number of shares that are exchanged, (b) whether the trade was initiated by a buyer or seller, and (c) some notion of the magnitude of the price change induced by the trade. The induced price change cannot be known with any precision, because that depends greatly on the tone of the market at the time of execution.

However, unless something goes terribly wrong in the execution, the type of trade and the identity of the trader will be carefully hidden from everyone except the principals and their trading agents.

Volatility driven by *price changes* associated with administrative and lower-order trading becomes a fog surrounding the market's real reactions to the changing economic environment, but for many, seeing patterns in the fog actually becomes the name of the game. Some even spend their time drawing pictures of stock price changes to better understand and predict patterns in price reactions to trades of all orders![4]

The result of this interactive dynamic is an unstable gale of reactive and interactive complexity and price-driven volatility.

VOLATILITY AND THE LEVEL OF STOCK PRICES

As it turns out, investors in the stock market are highly risk-averse. This risk-aversion doesn't manifest itself in the cross section of stock returns because it is overridden by overreaction to past records of success and failure of the underlying corporations. Growth stocks (more volatile) tend to be overpriced. Value stocks (less volatile) tend to be underpriced. Thus, when we look at the cross-sectional relationship between risk and returns, the more volatile stocks tend to have lower realized returns. It *looks* as though investors are risk-loving rather than risk-averse.

Although the risk-aversion is overridden in the cross section, we can see it clearly in the time-series relationship between the volatility of the market as a whole and the aggregate level of stock prices.

The existence of options to buy and sell the S&P 500 stock index enables us to compute what the market thinks its volatility is going to be over the life of the option contracts. The dominating factor in determining the value of an option is the volatility of the underlying asset the option is written on. Given the prices of the options and the value of the underlying asset (in this case the S&P 500), we can back out what the market thinks its volatility is going to be. Let's call this estimate of volatility the market's *implied volatility* (gray line).

Figure 11-1 shows the time series for the level of the S&P 500 and the market's implied volatility between January 1990 and May 2008. Note that the volatility is highly unstable (black line).

Figures 11-2A through 11-2C show that the market reacts negatively to increases in its volatility. The graphs plot daily percentage changes in implied volatility against percentage changes in the value of the S&P 500 stock index. For the entire period (Figure 11-2A), the coefficient of determination is .47. That means that nearly half the variability in the day-to-day return to the index can

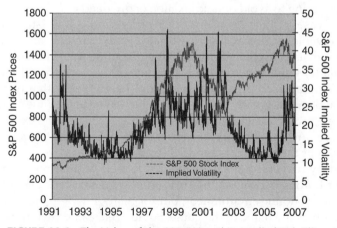

FIGURE 11-1 The Value of the S&P 500 and Its Implied Volatility

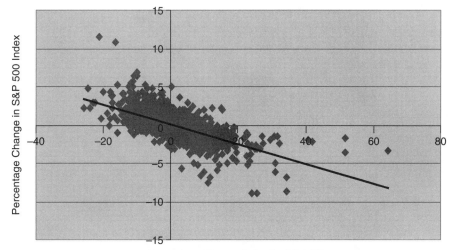

FIGURE 11-2A   Relationship Between Changes in Implied Volatility and Return to the S&P 500 (1/3/1990 to 2/23/2009)

be explained by changes in implied volatility! We're seeing the manifestation of the market's high level of risk-aversion in this graph. As implied volatility goes up, stockholders require a higher rate of return as compensation for their exposure to the higher level of volatility. Given the expected flow of future dividends, the only way to provide a higher return in the future is to lower the price now. Thus, increases in expected volatility (over the life of the S&P options) are associated with accompanying negative returns to the index.

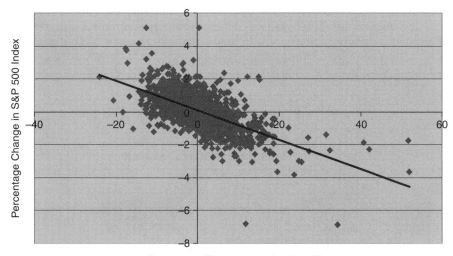

FIGURE 11-2B   Relationship Between Changes in Implied Volatility and Return to the S&P 500 (1/3/1990 to 7/19/1999)

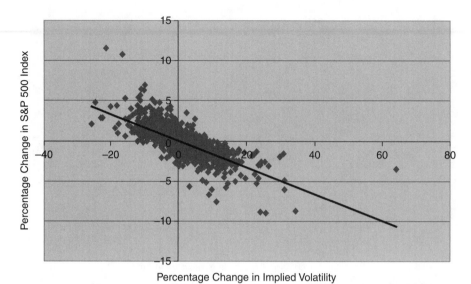

FIGURE 11-2C Relationship Between Changes in Implied Volatility and Return to the S&P 500 (7/20/1999 to 2/23/2009)

In Figures 11-2B and 11-2C, we divide the period into the front and back halves. The coefficients of determination are .37 for the back and .57 for the front . I would contend that, changes in market volatility are *the* most important determinant of daily stock returns.[5] In viewing these graphs, it's amusing to recall that supporters of efficient markets were able to "explain" the high returns on the less volatile value stocks and the low returns on the more volatile growth stocks by assuming that the market fears only fluctuation in aggregate dividends but is indifferent to changes in the price of risk. How do these authors explain what we now clearly see in Figures 11-2A through 11-2C?

It would be difficult to claim that the inherent instability in the time series of implied volatility can be accounted for by inherent instability in the underlying economic climate. Note, as indicated in Table 11-1, on seven occasions, the volatility of the stock market changed by more than 30% on a single day.

TABLE 11-1 Large Daily Changes in Market-Implied Volatility

Date	Percentage Change in Volatility
01/03/95	30.91%
01/27/95	−30.51%
08/25/95	34.17%
10/02/95	42.70%
06/03/96	31.63%
11/30/98	37.32%
11/20/00	38.54%

None of these days is particularly significant in U.S. history. The headlines appearing in Bloomberg on each of these days and the day preceding are provided in the appendix to this chapter. While the first volatility increase was associated with some concerns about inflation, a close look at these headlines, and the realization that they are all coincident with *major* shifts in the overall risk of the stock market, reveals how disconnected the market *is* from real-world events.

Note that the first trading day following September 11, 2001, is not included in the list. In fact, no day during the tumultuous War on Terror is included in this list, in spite of the fact that the U.S. economy is a prime terrorist target.

A true Zealot would claim that the day-to-day changes in implied volatility stem completely from day-to-day changes in the market's assessment of the underlying risk associated with economic and business conditions.

It is my contention that the implied volatility series is too unstable and too disconnected to real events to support the Zealots' view.

It seems more likely that implied volatility and the level of the stock index are mutually dependant, with implied volatility changing in accordance with the past sequence of changes in the price of the index, and the market index, in turn, reacting in a risk-averse manner to changes in the estimate of its own underlying volatility. *This, in my view, is the primary source of price-driven volatility*. There are other sources of volatility associated with price pattern recognition by technical analysts, or chartists, or the Dow passing through milestones like the 10,000 mark. However, these pale by comparison to price level adjustments associated with day-to-day changes in the market's learning process and changes in its assessment of its own volatility.

WHAT PERCENTAGE OF VOLATILITY IS PRICE-DRIVEN?

Based on the parade of evidence set forth in *Beast*, the fraction of total stock volatility induced by learning on the part of the market is normally quite high. The fraction stemming from rational or behavioral reactions to real events is likely to be quite small.

In this environment, some[6] may notice that the volatility of stock prices is excessive relative to the volatility of the surrounding economic climate. Few, however, recognize the dire implications of this excess volatility on the cost of equity capital and, ultimately, on long-run economic growth.[7]

Can the market right itself? Under what conditions (slack in the wire and shocks to the wire) would the aerialists eventually "learn the ropes," and stop watching each other?

While this is an interesting academic question, evidence indicates that after nearly 200 years of trading on the New York Stock Exchange, the "aerialists" haven't learned very much.

French and Roll[8] (FR) examine the variance (square of volatility) of stock prices during those Wednesdays (exchange holidays) for roughly half of 1968 when the New York Stock Exchange shut down to catch up on paperwork. They also examine the variance during election days when the market was also shut down.

You might ask, "How can FR compute the variance of return on days when the stock exchange is shut down?"

A statistician would tell you that, if the distribution of possible returns is constant from day to day, then the variance of returns measured over two-day intervals should be twice as large as the variance measured over one-day intervals. FR examine thousands of stocks, one at a time, and measure their variances using one-day returns. Then, for the exchange holidays, they compute the variance of returns from the close on Tuesday to the close on Thursday. In an efficient market, stock values should be moving in response to new information during the exchange holidays, even though they aren't being traded. The only pieces of information missing during those holidays are the stock prices themselves. If the distribution of possible returns during the holidays was the same as on other weekdays, the variance measured from Tuesday's close to Thursday's close should be twice as large as the one-day variance. But it wasn't. It was only 14% larger. FR perform similar calculations for election days. On average, across thousands of stocks, the variance was only 16% greater. They also calculate the weekly variance for weeks containing election days or exchange holidays. For election weeks, the variance was only 84% of that in normal weeks. For exchange holidays, it was only 82% as great. It's as though a fifth of the relevant pricing information is missing in those weeks during which the market is open for only four days.[9]

This evidence points strongly to the fact that the variance of return is much smaller during weekdays when the market is closed. On these exchange holidays and election days, the flow of information about real economic events is likely to be the same as on other weekdays. The only pieces of information not present during these days are stock price quotations. In an efficient market, these quotations should be irrelevant to the process of valuing the shares of corporations.

However, price quotations are the only source of information relevant to technical analysts (chartists). So this segment of the market ceases to influence pricing when the market shuts down. But, as discussed above, there is an influence much more important than this in explaining why the variance sharply dissipates on weekdays when the market shuts down.

The quotations may provide critical clues in the market's assessment of what its volatility is, and we know from Figure 11-2A through 11-2C that this assessment has a profound impact on daily stock returns. Shut down stock quotations and you shut down changes in the market's assessment of its own risk. Since changes in this assessment explains approximately half of the variability of daily stock returns (Figure 11-2A), if you shut down stock trading, you shut down the lion's share of stock price variability.

STOCK VOLATILITY AND STOCK MARKET COLLAPSES

Figure 11-3 shows a time series for the implied volatility[10] for the S&P 500 options contract during the time of the stock market crash of 1987. Note the explosion of (price-driven) volatility at the time of the October 19 crash. The Zealots don't like this graph.

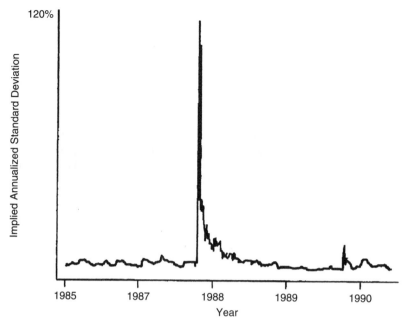

FIGURE 11-3 Implied Volatility in the Vicinity of the 1987 Crash

Despite its incredibly dramatic nature, the behavior of volatility around the crash is seldom discussed in the literature of financial economics. Why did the market's assessment of its volatility violently explode on October 19. Just as there are no apparent explanations for the large volatility increases of Table 11-1, there is no real economic event that could plausibly explain the explosion illustrated in Figure 11-3.

If, as the results of FR indicate,[11] the preponderance of stock volatility is price-driven, how is the market to learn about this component of its volatility if not by watching its own behavior and *learning*.

Figure 11-4 plots the time series of daily returns to the S&P 500 leading up to Tuesday, October 6, 1987. After experiencing this series, the market may come to believe that the probability distribution for its daily return might look like the bell-shaped curve at the end of the series.[12] In Table 11-2 we show the series of daily returns leading up to the catastrophic reassessment of volatility that occurred on October 19.

On Tuesday, October 6, the market fell by 2.7%. This would have to come from the left-hand tail of the probability distribution of Figure 11-4, but it probably wasn't unusual enough for the market to seriously re-evaluate its assessment of the nature of the underlying probability distribution. However, the sequence of returns coming on the 14th, 15th, and 16th could not realistically come from the probability distribution of Figure 11-4. So the market re-evaluates and sharply increases its assessment of its underlying volatility. Given the relationship shown in Figure 11-2A, this requires a sharply lower price level to provide higher *future* returns to compensate for the higher perceived risk.

So the market opens on Monday morning down 20%.

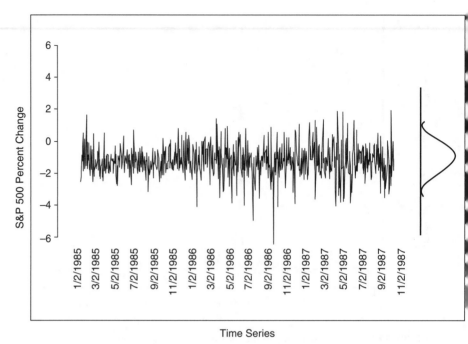

FIGURE 11-4   Stock Volatility January 1985 to September 1987

Adding this number to the bottom of Table 11-2 would seem to require a further re-evaluation of volatility, which would call for a further downward price adjustment. At the end of the day, the market's assessment of its volatility had risen to 120% as shown in Figure 11-3—all internally generated; all having nothing to do with real economic events.

HOW THE STOCK MARKET SPEAKS TO THE ECONOMY

It's well understood how the economy speaks to the stock market. "The unemployment rate rose by 0.2%; industrial production fell by 5%; etc." However, how the stock market talks to the economy is less well understood.

TABLE 11-2: Returns to the S&P 500 Prior to Oct. 19, 1987	
Tuesday, Oct. 6th	−2.70%
Wednesday, October 7th	−.22%
Thursday, October 8th	−1.37%
Friday, October 9th	−.99%
Monday, October 12th	−.54%
Tuesday, October 13th	1.66%
Wednesday, October 14th	−2.95%
Thursday, October 15th	−2.34%
Friday, October 16th	−5.16%

If the market were perfectly efficient, it would always be silent. The level of stock prices would always reflect current and future economic conditions to the extent they can be forecasted. Stock volatility would always reflect the level of uncertainty related to those real economic conditions. The information relevant to pricing stocks would exclusively be related to real economic events. The stock market would always reflect these and only these events. Beyond these events, there would be no additional information coming from an informationally efficient stock market.

However, an inefficient stock market is capable of generating news of its own. As we saw in the case of the 1987 crash, explosions in stock volatility can be internal to the stock market, un-triggered by real, external events. Increases in volatility can lead to reductions in the level of stock prices, as revealed in Figures 11-2A, 11-2B and 11-2C.

Endogenous increases in stock market volatility can present problems in and of itself. Increases in this volatility can create uncertainty on the part of consumers and corporate investors. As a consumer, you're planning to buy a car. But what kind of car should you buy—an economy car or something more luxurious? Increased uncertainty stemming from increased stock volatility increases (a) the probability of a poor choice and (b) the value of the option to wait until you see how the dust settles. The same is true of the corporate investor who manufactures the car. Should you expand capacity to manufacture luxury or economy cars? Should you expand at all? Again, increased uncertainty increases the value of the option to wait.

Increased uncertainty coming from increased stock volatility can result in reductions in corporate investment and consumer spending.

The reductions in the level of stock prices associated with higher stock volatility can also have destructive effects. Lower stock prices increase the cost associated with selling stock or even retaining earnings. This is because the higher volatility has increased the rate of return stockholders demand over the expected period of high volatility. Assume that the risk premium in expected stock returns is proportional to the variance.[13] An increase in stock volatility of 40% increases the variance by 16%, which, in the presence of the level of risk-aversion apparent in Figure 11-2A, can increase the cost of equity capital dramatically. In addition, there will be wealth effects on consumers who feel poorer as the value of their stock portfolios fall. An internally generated decline in stock prices can diminish consumption.[14]

In October of 1987, the U.S. economy was strong. So the violent disturbance in the stock market had little effect on gross domestic product. This time the conversation was one-way. The economy didn't talk back.

However, there were other times when we weren't so lucky.

STOCK VOLATILITY AND THE GREAT DEPRESSION

Figure 11-5 plots the daily rate of return to the Dow Jones Industrial Average in the vicinity of the Great Crash and on into the Great Depression. At the time, options on the index didn't exist, so we can't compute the market's implied

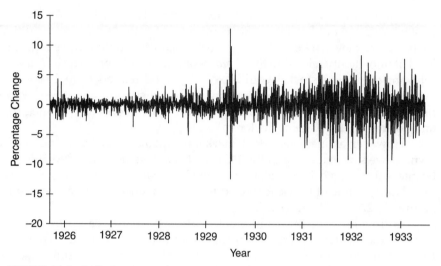

FIGURE 11-5 Daily Returns to the Dow Jones Industrials in the Vicinity of the Great Crash

volatility. However, it is obvious from the spread in returns that there was a marked increase in volatility in the last part of 1929. Unlike the 1987 experience, volatility continued to remain high throughout the early 1930s. This is, indeed, an example of a dangerous conversation where the market began talking to the economy and the economy began talking back.

As discussed above, the market talks to the economy through its volatility (by increasing uncertainty and the value of the option to wait to consume and invest as well as by increasing the cost of equity capital) and through its wealth effects. Unlike today, in 1929 very few people held common stocks, so the wealth effects can be dismissed as minimal. However, a reading of the *Wall Street Journal* from September 1929 through 1930 would verify that what was happening in the stock market was very much in the news. Toward the end of 1930, an exasperated Thomas Woodlock, a frequent contributor to the *Journal*, wrote the following:[15]

> "Nerves" are not confined to stock market circles. They are a contagious disease that tends to spread with rapidity and virulence to all circles of human activity. That the present mood of "Wall Street"—the phrase is used to specify the circles directly interested in the stock market— is infecting business in general, at least to some extent, is evident, and it is evident that the infection is spreading. More than one letter has been received by the *Wall Street Journal* urging either that dealings in stocks be suspended altogether or that quotations not be published! From this may be gleaned some idea of the riot of unreason that is loose in men's minds these days.

Some attribute the Great Depression to tight monetary policy.[16] However, monetary explanations fail to account for what was happening in 1930. In this year, the Federal Reserve actually lowered the discount rate three times from 5.0% to 3.5%.

In 1930, industrial production fell by a colossal 24%! Using monthly numbers for consumer durables spending and daily numbers to compute monthly stock volatility, Christina Romer, head of Barack Obama's council of economic advisors, modeled the relationship between stock volatility and durables spending in the United States between 1891 and 1928.[17] Based on the level of stock volatility that existed in 1930 (see Figure 11-5), her model predicted a decline in spending of 44% for the year. The actual decline turned out to be 32%.

As discussed above, higher stock volatility can also be expected to impact investment spending by corporations through its effect on uncertainty and the cost of equity capital. In fact, in 1930, investment spending fell by 35% relative to its value in 1929.[18]

In 1929, the stock market began talking to the economy, and in 1930, the economy began talking back—a dangerous conversation that ended in economic disaster. Stock volatility would remain high through 1934. The economy gradually recovered, but in 1937 the stock market struck again.

Figure 11-6 again charts the daily return to the Dow, this time from January 1935 through April 1938. Once again, on August 1, 1937, stock volatility exploded, sending stock prices plummeting. Prior to this second round of trouble in the stock market, the economy had been recovering, and safety nets such as federal deposit insurance had been put into place. The economy now faced a major setback with the explosion in stock volatility. After August, the manufacture of consumer durable goods fell by more than it did in 1930. By May 1938, the unemployment rate had risen back to 20%. Finally, in 1942, the United States became the second country to emerge from the Great Depression by mobilizing for war. You can guess which country was first.

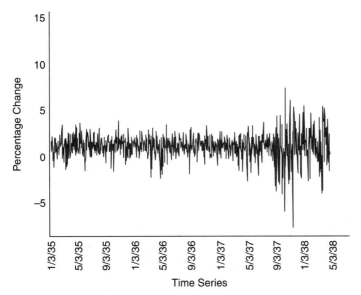

FIGURE 11-6   Daily Returns to the Dow Jones Industrials in the Vicinity of the Second Stock Market Crash

THE GREAT DEPRESSION AND THE RISE OF THE NAZI PARTY

Following its post–World War I battle with hyperinflation, the German economy appeared to have recovered nicely, with its unemployment rate reaching as low as 5% in 1925. However, with the passing of the Dawes plan the year before, the United States had become the major creditor-financier of (post–World War I) Europe. Propped up by extensive short-term loans to the United States, the German economy was actually in a rather fragile state.

In fact, shortly before his death in 1929, former German Chancellor and Foreign Minister Gustav Stresemann stated:

> The economic position is only flourishing on the surface. Germany is in fact dancing on a volcano. If short-term credits are called in, a large section of our economy would collapse.

After the Great Crash, most of these credits were called in, and the German economy, in fact, did collapse. As it turned out, of all countries in the world, Germany was the hardest hit by the Great Depression. Figure 11-7 plots the German unemployment rate (black bars) along with the percentage of the vote earned by the Nazi Party (gray bars). As the German unemployment rate rose to 30%, the popularity of the Nazis rose in lockstep. Those who weren't taken seriously before, took control of the government in 1932.

It seems that conventional wisdom has some merit after all.

THE FINANCIAL CRISIS OF 2008

It would seem that the conventional wisdom of the past has relevance for the present and the future. The effects of stock volatility on uncertainty are just as applicable today as they were in the past. The wealth effects of stock market activity are much more impactful now because a much higher percentage of the population owns stock than in 1930.

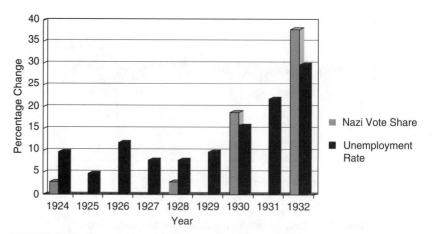

FIGURE 11-7 German Unemployment and Nazi Party Political Support

The length of the effective trading day is getting longer. Just as stock volatility declined with the exchange holidays of 1968, we can expect it to increase as the number of trading hours in the week becomes longer. Moreover, world equity markets are much more integrated today. A precipitous decline in the U.S. stock market can be expected to spread to other markets in a matter of hours. Today, there is no need to call in credits to spread economic problems.

The financial crisis of 2008 originated in the debt markets rather than the stock market. Fannie May and Freddie Mac were encouraged by Congress to inform banks that they stood ready to buy sub-prime loans. The banks, knowing they had a ready market to sell the sub-prime loans they issued, readily complied. This fueled the bubble in the housing market, and when housing prices turned down, the credit markets collapsed. The impact was felt far beyond traditional lenders because "toxic" mortgage backed securities now contaminated the books of financial institutions world wide. Congress' intention to increase the ratio of affordable housing backfired because they failed to consider the systemic effects of their directives. A coincident and unprecedented escalation in oil prices fueled the fire even more.

As once-acclaimed financial institutions began to crumble, stock volatility increased dramatically in September and broke through 80% in October. As expected, given Figure 11-2A, the stock market collapsed as well. As I sit in January, 2009 adding this section to the page proofs for the book, stock volatility is still triple its normal value—this, with its attendant effects on uncertainty, wealth levels, the cost of capital, investment and consumption. Unlike Figure 11-3, high stock volatility is persisting much as it did in 1930. The fact that this crisis didn't start with the stock market doesn't mean that the stock market isn't currently fully in charge of the situation. As discussed in footnote 14 to this chapter, the stock market has a monetary and fiscal policy of its own, the power of which transcends that of the Congress or the Federal Reserve.

On the eve of Barack Obama's inauguration, we can only hope that his economic team comes to the correct conclusions and recognizes the role of the stock market in the current crisis. Are we now in a dangerous conversation? We'll have to wait and see. Watch implied stock volatility and hope it comes down—soon![19]

Notes

1. See R. Haugen, *Beast on Wall Street: How Stock Volatility Devours Our Wealth* (Upper Saddle River, NJ: Prentice Hall, 1999).

2. R. Haugen, *The Inefficient Stock Market: What Pays Off and Why*, 2nd ed. (Upper Saddle River, NJ: Prentice Hall, 2001).

3. Or at least a sufficient number of investors that would result in an instantaneous and unbiased market price reaction to the information.

4. Thus, price impacts associated with the collective activity of chartists are among the sources of price-driven volatility. As we shall see in the next section, however, there is a *primary* source.

5. A similar analysis, with the same conclusion, was conducted on monthly percentage changes in the index by Cutler, Poterba, and Summers. See D. Cutler, J. Poterba, and L. Summers, *Journal of Portfolio Management* (1989).

6. R. Shiller, "Do Stock Prices Move Too Much To Be Justified by Subsequent Changes in Dividends?" *American Economic Review* (1982).

7. Haugen, *Beast on Wall Street*, p. 134.

8. See K. French and R. Roll, "Stock Return Variances: The Arrival of Information and the Reaction of Traders," *Journal of Financial Economics* (1986).

9. Some argue that, because the market was closed, influential traders, like Warren Buffet (whose trades, should he blow his cover, signal information about real economic events) were unable to signal with their trades. In this sense, these real information signals from informed investors stop when the market is closed. However, we can expect that the Warren Buffets of the world, who were prevented from trading on exchange holidays and on election days, would trade the day after. In this sense, the information that was embodied in their trades would have been released on Thursday or the day after the election. Thus, it would have been reflected in the variance of the two-day return or the variance of return for the entire week. But it wasn't.

10. The implied volatility of Figure 11-3 was calculated using at-the-money options, a binomial pricing framework and an estimated dividend stream over the life of the contract.

11. We should note that it isn't apparent to F&R, who are both efficient market devotees.

12. The probability distribution at the end of the series should be taken to be the market's assessment as of the last day of the series. You should assume, however, that this distribution is changing day-to-day and hour-to-hour as price changes occur.

13. This will be true for reasonable assumptions about investor utility of wealth.

14. Thus, the stock market seems to have a monetary and fiscal policy of its own. As the Federal Reserve changes the discount rate, the stock market may be countering by changing the cost of equity capital in the opposite direction. While Congress acts to lower taxes on income, the stock market may counter by lowering levels of wealth. These counter-moves by the stock market can be swamping.

15. T. Woodlock, *The Wall Street Journal*, November 10, 1930.

16. An exception would be P. Temin, *Did Monetary Forces Cause the Great Depression?* (New York: W. W. Norton, 1976).

17. C. Romer, "The Great Crash and the Onset of the Great Depression," *Quarterly Journal of Economics* (1990).

18. In the Great Crash and the Great Depression, we have two economic events with the word *Great* in their names. These events occurred within months of each other. Most economists would allege that the stock market saw the Great Depression coming. Read the issues of the *Wall Street Journal* published during the second half of 1929, and ask yourself if the market had a clue as to what was coming. The stock market didn't see the Great Depression coming; it *caused* it. And, for the most part, the stock market isn't a leading indicator because it anticipates economic events, but because it actively *causes* them.

19. You can track the market's implied volatility with this link: http://finance.yahoo.com/echarts?s=%5EVIX#symbol=%5EVIX;range=1y.

APPENDIX
HEADLINES FROM DAY OF AND DAY PRECEDING VOLATILITY SHIFTS

1/3/95

Headline News

Business and Finance Viacom close to selling cable systems for $2.2 bln

U.S. bonds fall as disappointing year closes

Spectrum Information soars after board quits, CEO named

Calif. Supreme Court upholds Advanced Micro chip rights

MCI files complaint against Pacific Bell

Hewlett-Packard to cut prices of its DeskJet printers

U.S. new home sales fell 2.5% in Nov.

Respironics receives warning letter from FDA

Ford CEO says rate hikes won't stall auto sales

Mexican peso falls amid skepticism about Zedillo plan

Virgin Air suit allowed to proceed against British Air

Orange County fund to sell $458 mln in securities

U.S. economy: purchasing managers' inflation index at 14-yr high

GOP to take control of Congress with long first day

Worldwide Two killed, 5 hurt in shootings at abortion clinics

Gingrich to turn down $4.5 million book advance

Mexico's Zapatistas will pull back troops

U.S. tells Haitians in Cuba they must leave

Italy's President Scalfaro rules out elections

Violence over new Israeli housing on West Bank

Russia, Chechnya still locked in battle

Crashed Turkish airliner's 'black box' recovered

Clinton orders police task force for abortion clinics

Iraq says 470 killed in fighting between rival Kurds

Israel's Peres regrets Gaza deaths, backs talks

1/27/95

Headline News

Business and Finance Teledyne to pay $3.9 mln in fines for helping Iraq

Fed Chairman Greenspan sees "torrid growth" slowing

McDonald's 4th-qtr net 43c-share vs 36c-share

GTE 4th-qtr profit rises 9.6% on cellular revenue

Procter & Gamble 2nd-qtr net $1.06-Share vs 92c-share

PaineWebber 4th-qtr net before Kidder 18c-share vs 72c

MCI 4th-qtr profit from ops 35c-share vs 34c

Coca-Cola 4th-qtr net 44c-share vs 36c-share

U.S. Economy: Durable Orders Surge to 16-Year High

U.S. economy grew at 4.5% rate in 4th-qtr; 4% in 1994

U.S. bonds extend gain after GDP report; 30-yr at 7.78

Time Warner to acquire Houston Industries cable unit

Gingrich won't say if Mexico aid bill will be approved

Lockheed to pay $24 mln in Egyptian bribery case

Hershey 4th-qtr net 29c-share with charge vs $1.04

Stop & Shop raided in FBI food-industry probe

Dollar slips on concern about approval of Mexican aid

USAir 4th-qtr loss $5.63-share vs loss $2.29-share

Texas Instruments 4th-qtr net rises 40% to $1.98-share

Worldwide Utah man arrested for threats against Clinton, Gore

Clinton tells mediator to get baseball talks going

State Department denies Bosnian group altered plan

PLO, Jordan agree on cooperation, Jerusalem shrines

Jewish group boycotts Auschwitz liberation ceremony

North Korea rejects Seoul's proposal for talks

Israelis arrest 30 in raid on West Bank college

Russian mothers win release of 6 Chechnyan soldiers

Bosnian fighting at worst level in four months

U.S. exhibit on Hiroshima bomb may be cancelled

8/25/95

Headline News

Business and Finance IBM signs licensing agreement for Windows 95

Novell shares fall after disappointing 3rd-qtr profit

AlliedSignal to buy Northrop Grum-man unit

U.S. economy: durables tumble on car plant closures

Thursday's U.S. markets: bonds rise on signs of slower growth

Enron unit makes $196.8 mln bid for Coda Energy

Bertelsmann seeks partner in America Online venture

Ford Bronco II Rollover Verdict Cut

South Western accepts Southern Co.'s increased bid

Medaphis general counsel resigns amid

ABC News' bias damages rejected by appeals court

Philadelphia Fed survey sees 3rd-qtr inflation at 2.9%

Cordis 4th-qtr earnings rise before suit settlement

U.S. economy: mow mortgages bolster July home resales

Republic Waste to acquire Southland Environmental

Friday's U.S. Markets: Bonds Soar, Stocks Rise, Dollar Slides

Worldwide China expels U.S. activist Wu after spy conviction

U.N. Ukrainian peacekeepers leave Gorazde

U.S., Britain won't support lifting Iraq oil ban

Zaire stops forced expulsion of refugees from camps

Israel, Palestinians reach water agreement

India optimistic Kashmir rebels to release hostages

Danish court approves extraditing American neo-nazi

Bermuda selects finance minister David Saul as premier

U.S. First Lady to attend Beijing women's conference

Packwood seeks public hearings on misconduct charges

Egypt's Mubarak offers asylum to Saddam Hussein

British U.N. troops begin pullout from Gorazde

Croats, Serbs agree on ceasefire in East Slavonia

Two Hamas fugitives killed in Israeli shootout

China expels 2 journalists accused of spying

Fire burns thousands of acres in Long Island, New York

10/02/95

Headline News

Business and Finance Dollar rebounds as Swiss calls franc overvalued

Gartmore shares soar on possible bidding war

Forte to sell U.S. Travelodge hotel chain

New Jersey to drop high-oxygen gasoline rules

Tracinda hires activist to woo Chrysler holders

AT&T planned split spurs talk of Baby Bell link

U.S. Economy: New Home Sales Fell 9.6% in August

Friday's U.S. Markets: U.S. Bonds Post Biggest Gain in 5 Weeks

Mergers Surge to $564 bln in 9 Months, Nearing Record

Lucas to pay $88 mln to settle Pentagon dispute

Foster Wheeler seals Ahlstrom purchase, to cut 500 jobs

U.K. fraud office might enter Leeson case, then drop it

AT&T shelves interactive-TV for lack of interest

Fed puts restrictions on Daiwa Bank's New York branch

Tracinda's York says Daimler may buy 20% of Chrysler

Mexico's Bolsa stock index closes down 4.19%

Chrysler sales off 7% in Sept., General Motors up 0.5%

Monday's U.S. markets: bonds, dollar rise and stocks fall

U.S. economy: manufacturing index below expectations

Worldwide Wilson drops out of 1996 Republican presidential race

Clinton meets Congress leaders on Bosnia troop moves

Holbrooke returns to Sarajevo to push peace accord

Olajuwon hurts back, cancels $1 mln 1-on-1 with O'Neal

Gingrich breaks ranks to back ethanol subsidy

U.S. airport security tighter after sheik's conviction

Japan may recall ambassador after French nuclear test

Philippine storm deaths rise to 45 after landslide

6/3/96

Headline News

Business and Finance Chrysler violated California's lemon law, judge rules

Ascend Communications to buy NetStar for $300 mln

Germany's KHD working with Deutsche Bank on rescue

Japan jobless rate rises to 3.4% in April from 3.1%

U.S. economy: manufacturing up while spending is weak

Chrysler sales jump 17% in May on rebates, minivans

Justice opposes Union Pacific–Southern Pacific merger

Clear Channel to buy Heftel Broadcasting for $336 mln

Avis in talks to be acquired; HFS said to be suitor

Republic's Huizenga to sell 50% stake in Florida Panthers

Dutch Pakhoed to bid $303 mln for rest of Univar

IMF, Venezuela clear path for $3 bln in new loans

Worldwide Netanyahu beats Peres to become Israeli prime minister

LSD guru Timothy Leary, 75, dies of cancer

Japan, South Korea to co-host 2002 Soccer world cup

Italy's new government wins confidence vote

Clinton announces renewal of China's MFN trade status

EU finance ministers split on debt, currency criteria

Bahrain arrests 29 charged in Iran-backed coup plot

NATO to refashion links into leaner post–Cold War alliance

11/30/98

Headline News

Business and Finance U.S. stocks rise, led by oil, technology shares; Nasdaq sets high

U.S. bonds rise, pushing yields to a 4-week low, as dollar gains

Dollar sets a two-month high vs. mark on European rate cut hints

Record-setting rally just might have legs: U.S. stocks outlook

U.S. stocks suffer biggest loss in 2 months on profit concern

Crude oil falls as OPEC fights over output cuts

U.S. bonds surge as stocks fall; scant inflation seen

Worldwide Clinton to meet with Arafat Monday to draft economic aid request

Germany won't seek extradition of Kurdish leader, Schroeder says

Indian train wreck leaves 189 people dead, according to reports

Republican support for Clinton censure rises, *New York Times* says

U.S. FDA issues rule requiring company drug testing in children

Clinton urges tougher Internet self-regulation, seeks faster Web

Clinton to ask Congress to boost Palestinian aid by $400 million

Russia delays to Dec. 10 consideration of 1999 state budget

U.S. High Court won't rule on disposal of spent nuclear fuel

Quebec separatists need big victory for new secession vote

11/20/00

Headline News

Business and Finance ING Hires Goldman for Review of ING Barings Investment Bank Unit in U.S.

U.S. Says It's Gaining Support from OPEC for Oil Price of $20–$25 a Barrel

European Technology Shares May Decline This Week on Concern About Profits

U.S. Trade Deficit Likely Widened in September as Oil Rose, Analysts Say

Home Depot, Wal-Mart Expected to Be Top Appliance Sellers, Analysts Say

European Economy Reports to Show Slower Growth; German Confidence to Fall

Royal KPN Raises $4.7 Billion Through Sale of Shares, Convertible Bonds

British Pound May Decline Against the Dollar as Growth in U.K. Moderates

Telefonica May Need to Lower Price for IPO of Moviles Unit, Investors Say

Deutsche Post Prices Shares; IPO Values German Post Office at $20 Billion

Holiday Buyers Seek DVD, MP3 Players Amid Shortage of Sony's PlayStation

Steel Internet Exchanges Slow to Find Sales, Profit; Few Likely to Survive

U.S. Stocks Decline as Juniper Networks Drops; Nasdaq Hits 13-Month Low

Juniper Networks, Redback Fall as Morgan Stanley Cuts Computer Networking

Oracle Drops 14% After Company Loses Its Second Top Executive This Year

Agilent Technologies Says Fiscal Fourth-Quarter Profit More Than Doubles

Yen Drops to Eight-Month Low as Government Seen Distracted From Economy

America Online, Time Warner Delay Merger Completion After EarthLink Accord

Coca-Cola Shares Decline on Concern It Will Pay Too Much for Quaker Oats

Fifth Third Bancorp to Buy Old Kent for $4.75 Billion to Expand in Midwest

Heating Fuel Prices Surge as Cold U.S. Weather Erodes Already Low Supplies

DaimlerChrysler Fires Chrysler Sales Chief Cunningham and Two Other Execs

EBay Shares Decline 21% After Lehman Analyst Cuts Rating on Slower Sales

Cash Declines as Takeover Currency, Squeezing Buyers, Amid Junk-Bond Slump

Worldwide Florida County's Ballot Recount Could Take 10 Days or More, Officials Say

Peru's President Fujimori to Resign, Ending More Than a Decade in Power

Yahoo Faces Fines in French Court for Allowing Web Access to Nazi Items

Austria Hit by Avalanches; Two Dead, at Least Two Missing, AFP Reports

Seagram's *Grinch* Opens as No. 1 Film With $55.1 Million, Tops *Rugrats*

Florida Justices Seek Deadline for Limiting Presidential Vote Recounts

Japanese Prime Minister Mori Survives No-Confidence Vote in Parliament

Israeli Helicopters Hit Palestinian Targets in Gaza After Bus Bombing

Yahoo Must Block Nazi Site Access or Face a Daily Fine, Paris Court Rules

American Air Attendant Dies, Three Hurt After Emergency Landing in Miami

CHAPTER **12**

Rational Finance,
Behavioral Finance,
and the New
Finance

THE NEW FINANCE

Some may question how this work can be distinguished from the increasingly popular area of behavioral finance.

In my mind, this book embraces themes that coincide with some of the paradigms of behavioral finance. However, while behavioral finance focuses on the peculiarities of human behavior and their implications for asset pricing, I believe that the New Finance extends to issues beyond these concepts.

Some advocates of behavioral finance take a more informal approach, suggesting that behavioral tendencies, taken from psychological literature, might serve to explain anomalies that are empirically observed in the financial markets.[1] Others take a more rigorous approach. They modify purely rational preference functions in mathematical asset pricing models so that the predictions from closed-form solutions to these models are more consistent with the anomalies than models based on purely rational preferences.[2]

Both approaches begin with assumptions about the behavior of individuals, assume uniformity in aspects of the nature of this behavior, aggregate across individuals, and end with predictions about the structure of the prices of financial assets.

The Theory, for example, assumes that all individuals hold efficient portfolios. Then it aggregates to get the prediction that the market index will be efficient as well.

Both the rational and the behavioral approaches are fundamentally flawed because they fail to account for the *complexity* and the *uniqueness* of behavioral interactions on ultimate outcomes.

RATIONAL AND BEHAVIORAL ECONOMIC MODELS

In Economics 101, students may learn little about the length of the short run.

However, they do learn a simple and elegant microeconomic model about the determination of prices in a marketplace. Figure 12-1 shows the supply and demand curves for some asset, product, or service. Suppliers supposedly face rising marginal costs. To maximize profits, they keep producing (and supplying) until the marginal cost of producing one more unit is equal to the selling price. For any one supplier, there is a rising supply curve. As price goes up, as we aggregate over each individual supplier, the overall quantity supplied increases, and we have a rising total supply curve.

Consumers supposedly gain pleasure (utility) in consuming the product, which competes with others. Holding the nature and the price of these other products constant, consider the effect of changing the price on how much is demanded. As each individual consumer acquires more, he or she begins to become satiated. With each purchase, the utility associated with the new acquisition goes down. To maximize total utility, rational consumers must keep buying until the marginal utility of the last purchase is equal to the price. As the price falls, the consumer is induced into the market to buy more, so as to match the marginal utility with the lower price. For any one consumer there is a falling demand curve, where the consumer wants more as the price goes down. Aggregating across all consumers, we obtain the total demand curve pictured in Figure 12-1.

Thus, we obtain a downward-sloped total demand curve—rising demand with falling prices.

Suppose we start at a low price in Figure 12-1. Here, consumers want to buy more than suppliers want to provide. Consumers raise the price they are willing to pay, which closes the gap, partially because producers offer more at the higher price. Price keeps rising to the point where the curves intersect. At the intersection of supply and demand, we are at equilibrium.[3] Supply is equal to demand, and nothing that is endogenous to the model will induce a further price change. Change must be induced by something exogenous—the introduction of a new, competing product, which changes the demand curve, or a change in production technology, which changes the supply curve.

In this simple, orderly model, everyone makes rational decisions so as to maximize total profits or total utility. Refer to this type as a *rational economic model.*

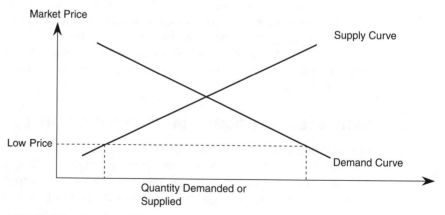

FIGURE 12-1 Supply and Demand Curves

The Theory is one example of a rational economic model.

It isn't that difficult to move to a *behavioral economic model* and account for the impact of irrational decisions on market price. For example, you can focus on the nature and determination of the marginal utility of consumption. In a rational model, consumers consider the properties of the product and how ownership of an additional unit will affect their marginal utility.

But let's impose some irrationality here.

Suppose the consumer takes the price, itself, as a signal of quality. Assume consumers have limited information concerning quality. Faced with two products that are seemingly the same, they may wish to assume that the product with the higher price is of higher quality. No problem for a behavioral economist. Just amend the utility function to make utility an endogenous function of price.

We now have a behavioral, but *orderly*, model.

In the presence of consumer behaviors that might be classified as less than rational, the demand curve must be adjusted accordingly. Conceivably, in a behavioral economic model, demand might even rise with price for a while, before satiation sets in.

But let's add some interaction and make things a little more *complex.*

In the simple, rational model of Figure 12-1, as price falls, more consumers enter the market. The identity of these consumers is irrelevant to the rational analysis of Figure 12-1. But suppose the entrance into the market by some consumers affects the demand of others. Suppose also that the consumers affected don't regard others equally. Some of them may be perceived to be more intelligent; some may possess more prestige, wealth, and power. Entrance into the marketplace by these individuals may provide signals about the quality or desirability of the product to others. Acquisitions by these individuals may change the perceived utility of the product to others.

"If *they* have this, *I* should have it too."

Behavioral economic models can be simple and orderly, but even the relatively simple interactive behaviors discussed above can become very complex.

Take those well-regarded consumers who enter the market. Surely they aren't equally well regarded by all others. They may be known by some but not by all. The desire to emulate may differ from consumer to consumer. Emulation might even be catchy! Do these people physically meet in the market place? How do their interactions affect mutual regard and perceptions of product quality?[4]

Orderly interactions are rare.

As we shall see, interactions between real things and real people tend to be highly *complex.*

ORDER, COMPLEXITY, AND CHAOS

Order *is* rare; complexity is everywhere.

It would initially appear the moon orbits the earth and the earth orbits the sun in a well-defined, orderly fashion. Order enables precise predictions of the tides and the timing of lunar and solar eclipses—at least in the short term. However, did you know that the accuracy of these predictions wanes as you extend the predictive horizon? Predictions millions of years out are imprecise. Predictions billions of years out are impossible.

Why?

There are thousands of massive objects in our solar system. These objects exercise gravitational forces on the moon, the earth, and even the sun. In the short term, the impact of these forces is negligible. However, after the passage of considerable time, what was negligible accumulates to something significant. In the very long run, the interactions between all of these objects dissolve into a sea of chaos, and predictions of relative position become impossible.

Now consider a globular cluster of millions of stars. Each star significantly interacts, even in the short term, with stars nearby. Those stars, in turn, interact with those in proximity to *them*. In the face of this interactive complexity,[5] predicting future relative position even over short periods becomes untenable.

What about the interactions between millions of human beings participating in the markets for stocks?[6]

Can the individual interactions be modeled to make meaningful predictions about the implications of their collective behavior on the stock price?

Given the present state of mathematics, the *complexity* of the interactions is an insurmountable problem in and of itself. However, it is the *uniqueness* of the interactions that is also ultimately fatal to standard economic models.

Each individual interaction must be taken as completely unique from all others.

To see why, first picture in your mind a triangle with a horizontal base and sides of equal length. Now draw a circle around the triangle, where the circle touches each of the three points. Beginning at any one of the points, move one-third of the way down the side and then 60 degrees (relative to the side) up to the circle. Now drop a straight line back to the side, two-thirds of the distance from the original point to the next. After repeating for the other two sides, you have a six-pointed Star of David, all points touching the circle.

Although the star still resides within the circle, the perimeter around the star is one-third greater than the perimeter around the original triangle.

Now begin again at any point of the star. Move a third of the way down the side, up 60 degrees, and then back to the side at two-thirds of its length. Repeat for each of the 12 sides of the star. The new object still resides with the circle, yet has a perimeter one-third greater than the Star of David. Repetition of this process results in an expansion of the perimeter by one-third each time. Conceptually, we can repeat infinitely, moving toward an object with an infinitely long perimeter but still residing within the circle.[7]

Continuing, we can ask, "What is the length of the perimeter around a *real* object?"

That length depends on the length of your ruler or how precisely you measure.

Tear a piece of paper so that it is roughly circular. What is the distance around? A one-inch measuring stick may circle the paper 20 times, point to point—a 20-inch perimeter.

But the paper isn't *perfectly* round. There are *irregularities* in real objects. A tenth-inch measuring stick captures some of these and may circle the paper

250 times—a 25-inch perimeter. As your ruler becomes even smaller, more irregularities come into play. You find that the distance around the paper increases without limit as your ruler becomes smaller and the precision of measurement increases.

The nature of your trip around the parameter and your sense of the paper's shape will be *unique* to the length of your measuring stick![8]

Actually, the limit to the *true* distance around any real, two-dimensional object is the limit of the measuring stick. If the stick can be infinitely small, the distance is infinitely large.

Now consider the fact that the thought experiment above, carried out for the triangle in the circle, also applies in three dimensions. In this case, visualize a four-sided pyramid imbedded so that each of its four points touches a sphere. We can retrace the steps above, now in three dimensions, to build a conceptual object with infinite surface area, still imbedded within the sphere.[9]

Just as the perimeter around any real two-dimensional object is infinite, the *area* of the surface of any real, three-dimensional object is also infinite.

The conceptual triangles and pyramids discussed above are not unique because they are perfectly *regular.*

Real objects are *irregular.*

Given any two real objects, if you can examine them with unlimited precession, you will find areas that are irregular and nonconforming.

Over all the "paper circles" you can possibly tear, no two will be *exactly identical.*

Real objects are *unique.*

By the same reasoning, interfaces and interactions between uniquely distinguishable objects are themselves unique, with each interaction peculiarly defined by the unique nature of the interface.

Outcomes of complex interactions between unique agents can't be aggregated or generalized. Each outcome is as unique as the reacting "surfaces" of the interfacing agents. Economists will attempt to enrich their models by capturing the interactions of individuals with greater precision. As with the globular cluster, with millions of market participants, this effort is rendered mathematically intractable by complexity and meaningless by uniqueness.

The mere perception of any given interface will change *without limit* with the precision of measurement.

Individually, the complex and unique interactions between heterogeneous agents cannot be modeled or aggregated in a meaningful way to explain or predict the eventual, collective outcomes on market pricing.

Two traders meet on the floor of the stock exchange. They are both agents acting on behalf of undisclosed principals. In the context of the framework set forth in this chapter, the principals, themselves, may actually be interacting after one observes the price impact of one or the other's previous trade. The principals, however, may have no knowledge of their *personal interactions.* Individually, they are only reacting to observed changes in market prices. The principals' agents now confront, and they attempt to communicate to make a trade.

Let's limit our analysis to the visual part of this interface. The interface may be face to face or through electronic media.

For one trader, light is received by the eyes and converted to electrical impulses, which are sent to the brain's visual cortex. Here, an analysis is performed on space, orientation, form, and color. This analysis is then passed on to other areas of the cortex that integrate the visual and auditory parts of the communication. The integrated information is then passed through the *arcuate fasciculus*, a pathway that connects a large network of interactive brain areas involved in language processing, cognition, association, and word meaning.

Each point of this process is unique.

Eventually, the interaction results in a trade and a possible change in price. But an attempt to aggregate from specific notions of the behavior of individual traders to the collective behavior and stock pricing, without considering the complexity and uniqueness of the interactions, would seem overly simplistic at best and *meaningless* at worst.

Of course, one can make the *gargantuan* assumption that the process always results in a *rational* response that maximizes utility of wealth. Unfortunately, the gargantuan assumption doesn't help the situation at all. Because, even with it in place, we are dealing with relative *perceptions* that are *unique, unto themselves*, and therefore cannot be aggregated.

The rational and behavioral economic models discussed above are posed in the context of an orderly environment. The myriad of unique interactions in the market place leads to the *complexity* that lies between *order* and *chaos*.

Chaos aficionados sometimes use the example of smoke from a cigarette rising from an ashtray. The smoke rises in an orderly and predictable fashion in the first few inches. Then the individual particles, each unique, begin to interact. The interactions become important. Order turns to complexity. Complexity turns to chaotic turbulence. Predicting the behavior of the smoke two feet above the ashtray is impossible.

The unique nature of the many individual particles makes their complex interactions, and ultimately the path of the smoke, totally unpredictable.[10]

Remember, the true area in any part of the brain is infinite and unique everywhere. The collective processing of information by brains cannot be meaningfully modeled. Even if you attempt to impose homogeneity through the assumption of rational response, heterogeneity in *perceptions* of common impulses of information implies that, even then, these responses are unique.

And so are the interactions.

How then to understand and predict the behavior of an interactive system of traders and their agents?

Not by taking a *micro* approach, where you focus on the behaviors of individual agents, assume uniformity in their behaviors and mathematically calculate the collective outcome of these behaviors.

Aggregation will take you *nowhere*.

Instead, take a macro approach. Observe the outcomes of the interaction—market-pricing behaviors. Search for tendencies *after* the dynamics of the interactions play themselves out.

View, understand, and then predict the behavior of the macro environment as we did in Chapter 10, rather than attempting to go from assumptions about micro to predictions about macro. *This* is the touchstone of the New Finance.

The market is in such a constant state of complex interaction that no individual behavior, rational or irrational, can be aggregated, modeled, or generalized under an assumption of a fixed set of external conditions.

SCALING THE STOCK MARKET

Each point on the scale depicted in Figure 12-2 represents a possible state of the stock market. The scale measures the fraction of stock volatility that is price driven. At the extreme left-hand side, we have the rare state of order in any system, where there are no price effects associated with unique and complex investor interactions. As you begin to move to the right on the scale, you begin to experience the effects of investor interactions on pricing. Here complexity sets in. Finally, at the extreme right we have complete turbulence and utter chaos. There, all stock volatility is price driven, and price changes are completely unrelated to changes in the real economic information set.

Price-driven volatility accounts for *all* of the action. Real economic events are irrelevant to *this* market.

While each point on the scale represents a conceivable state for a market, the market's condition in this regard need not be stationary. Since, as we know from Chapter 11, the fraction of volatility that is price-driven is unstable, the position of the real market slides on the scale as time passes.

Rational and behavioral models that don't account for the effects of unique and complex interactions work best in hypothetical markets positioned to the extreme left. Market efficiency is a rational, special case of the extreme left. The irrational behaviors accounted for in game-theoretic or non-interactive, behavioral models are associated with states of market inefficiency, but they are still positioned at the extreme left.

The impacts of interaction through the interpretation of signals in channels of information is introduced as soon as you move right on the scale.

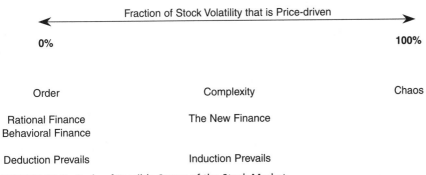

FIGURE 12-2 Scale of Feasible States of the Stock Market

The number, the nature, and the effect of these interactions on price volatility is based on (a) the number of trades, (b) the dollar volume of trading, (c) the relative liquidity of stock prices, and (d) the length of clock time over which trades are executed.[11]

It's not clear how quickly increasing the intensity of interactions causes you to approach the extreme right. Indeed, it's not clear if 100% is even a possibility.

Again, as we travel from left to right, we go from order to complexity and finally into chaos.

At the extreme left, where there is order, mathematical models may predict and explain well.

As we move to the right, *induction* and statistical estimation dominate *deduction* and mathematical modeling in their ability to explain and predict.

Recognition of the folly of deductive, mathematical microeconomic modeling in the face of complex interaction is another touchstone of the New Finance.

Induction dominates deduction in its predictive power.

Observing the macro behavior of markets rather than going from assumptions about the micro behavior of individuals to predictions about macro pricing.

Financial economists, both rational and behavioral, dazzle themselves with sophisticated mathematics. They gain much comfort in the intellectual rigor of their methodologies.

It makes no difference if their assumptions are completely unrealistic, *so long as they parallel those made by their peers.*

To them, elegance is all that matters. They look with disdain on the studies of psychologists, sociologists, and anthropologists because their work seems so mushy in comparison to their own. They dismiss, as unimportant, forces that may actually be *crucial* but impossible to treat with mathematical rigor.

Mathematical models can do a fair job at predicting the path of an arrow shot into the air.

But these models fail utterly in predicting the path of something, flying with feathers, that is alive and processing and storing information and flying in response. Is the flying rational and optimum? How much of the environment is seen? How is it perceived? How much is rationally processed? How much of the behavior of other fliers is perceived? How much is copied? Is nearly everything based on dynamics and surprise? As flyers flock and interact, can *any* part of their environment be taken as fixed (as we did with aspects other than price in the demand curve of 12-1) in attempting to model any aspect of flight?

Does a mathematical economist really know what it means to be spontaneous and alive?

Suppose you wanted to develop a process that would find birds. Would anyone really expect that deduction would outpower induction? Ornithologists don't use mathematical models of individual bird behavior to help them explain bird behavior. Instead, they look based on data passed down from others. Their search procedures are almost completely based on *induction*.

Similarly, in searching for mispriced stocks in highly interactive, complex, and sometimes even chaotic markets, it is best to set aside the mathematical models of the rational and behavioral financial economists. These models may be admired for their rigor, their beauty, and their elegance. They may win prizes, but alas, they are without foundation.

They have *no* power to explain or predict.

Yes, they are elegant. And, they are beautiful. But they are *empty*.

Bet on the black belt in a fight with the body builder. His opponent trains only to look good and he's bound to *lose*.

In your fight to win in the stock market, set the deductive, mathematical models and theories aside and rely, instead, on induction. Come to this complex, interactive, and inefficient market *unburdened* by predisposition.

Cast your net widely, and let statistics and econometrics guide your predictions.

THE TOOL IS COOL . . .

It would be wrong to be *too* critical of economics. Much of economic thought serves as an important guide to getting things done right.

The Tool, for example, shows us how to build efficient portfolios. Market-neutral hedge funds use commercial versions of The Tool to build high-return–low-risk portfolios of hundreds of stocks. Roughly half of these stocks are borrowed and then sold short. The proceeds of these sales are then invested in a risk-free asset like treasury bills. The short portfolio is matched with a portfolio where the stocks are held long. The Tool is used to select the long and short stocks so that the volatility of the *differences* in the returns to the two portfolios is minimized, while maximizing the spread between their expected returns. The Tool is a truly powerful way to make money.

There is also much to learn from the theory of the finance of the firm. There are tax benefits to financing with debt because interest payments are deductible. The presence of debt in capital structures also creates incentives for equity owners to take on investments with excessive risk. It's important to know the implications in selling or buying corporate debt. Using debt properly is also a powerful way to make money.

The same is true for selling debt by the government. Politicians warn of the dire implications of the national debt on our kids. But the economics of public finance teaches us to think deeper about our kids. Suppose, for example, that the government decides to issue $1,000 more government bonds instead of taxing you the $1,000 directly. Worried about the implications for your kids, because the government must eventually tax your kids to repay the bonds? If you're really concerned, then take the $1,000 you'd otherwise pay in taxes and *buy* the bonds instead. Then your kids can cash in the bonds to pay their taxes with no problem.

Should you really believe that the national debt is a disaster waiting to happen?

You see, we all can gain considerable insight from economics.

But be leery of the theories.

This book warns to be skeptical of theories that go from how individuals *should* behave to the supposed impact of their aggregated behaviors on things such as market prices.

Psychologists teach us about the behavior of *individuals*. Sociologists teach us about the behavior of *groups*. Sociologists don't aggregate.

"What's the best possible way to build a house?" will not get you to an accurate prediction of the ultimate nature of cities.

It would seem that economists are rather unique in following their path from the micro to the macro.

Individual behavior cannot be generalized to predict *interactive* group and pricing behavior.[12]

THE NEW CORPORATE FINANCE

From the first page to the last, the propositions set forth in a standard corporate finance text are founded in the context of efficient financial markets.

To maximize wealth, a financier should behave very differently in an *inefficient* market. What is the right way to make money in an inefficient market?

In the context of the New Finance, management should operate in the following general investment/financing decision framework.

In considering the costs of raising capital through their firm, managers should employ state-of-the-art *inductive* technology (supplemented with their own inside information) to forecast the expected returns to their firm's menu of prospective securities that can be used to finance their investments. *Given the complexity of the interactions of market participants, this technology should not be based on theories derived from modeling micro behaviors.*

Forecasts of the cost of capital should be based on statistical models that measure macro tendencies in the behavior of stock market prices.

Management should rely on technology that is truly state of the art in terms of its power to predict future returns *out of sample.*

In financing their firms, managers should determine the least-expensive bundle of securities that can be issued. As long as the firm's assets are mispriced by the market (over- *or* undervalued), the firm should be able to create security bundles that are *overvalued.* In finding the least-expensive bundle, it matters not what the firm's security holders expected the returns to be or even what they want them to be. *What counts is what management believes they are going to be.*

Next, management should consider its investment alternatives both in the real sector and in the financial sector. Remember, *in the inefficient market,* armed with state-of-the-art expected return statistical models, management may see investments with very high rates of return in the financial markets. Management's own stock may be one of these, but it is special only in the context of management's private information and the fact that it is a tax-free investment. These financial expected returns should be compared with alternatives in the real sector.

In a tax-free world, assuming away attendant problems associated with mutually exclusive investments, issues of signaling, agency problems, and other factors that create interdependence between the investment and financing decision, management should opt for the investment with the highest risk-adjusted expected return, *provided the returns are higher than the expected returns on the lowest-cost bundle of securities used to finance.*

Management should continue its external financing and investing until the gap between the risk-adjusted expected returns to the investments and the lowest-cost source of finance closes. For investments internally financed, management should accept projects that have expected returns greater than the greater of those expected and required by its stockholders or that expected by management.

Following this path, stockholder wealth will be maximized.

Notes

1. W. DeBondt and R. Thaler, "Does the Stock Market Overreact?" *Journal of Finance* (July 1985).

2. Priming occurs when exposure to a stimulus affects a later response to a similar stimulus. Some have worked with modified utility functions where utility derived from current consumption depends on a habitual level of consumption. See, for example, S. Sundaresan, "Intertemporally Dependant Preferences and the Volatility of Consumption and Wealth," *Review of Financial Studies* (1996); and G. Constantinides, "Habit Formation: A Resolution of the Equity Premium Puzzle," *Journal of Political Economy* (1990).

3. In the efficient stock market, supply and demand are assumed to be infinitely elastic at the rationally determined market price. If the actual stock price falls slightly below the rational price, demanders literally pour money into the market for the stock. Conversely, at a slightly higher price, sellers flood the market. In an efficient market, Bill Gates can liquidate all his shares of Microsoft today at today's price. In this context, he really *is* as rich as they say he is!

4. In game-theoretic economic models, interactions by various participants in the model are explicitly considered. However, responses to the interactions are based on rationality. Moreover, conditioned by the wealth level and information set possessed by a given player, the nature of the responses is identical. The discussion set forth in this chapter is based entirely on the notion that, even with identical stimuli, each (rational or behavioral) response can be expected to be completely *unique*. Indeed, the stimuli, themselves, are likely to be individually unique. In this context, aggregation from individual behaviors to a collective solution, of any sort, is *meaningless*.

5. For discussions of the concept of complexity in economics see P. Anderson, K. Arrow, and D. Pines, eds., *The Economy as an Evolving Complex System* (Reading, MA: Addison-Wesley, 1988).

6. The price-driven component of stock volatility discussed in Chapter 11 is a product of investor interaction.

7. This is called the Koch curve, after Helge von Koch who first described it.

8. See B. Mandelbrot, "How Long Is the Cost of Britain? Statistical Self-Similarity and Fractional Dimension," *Science* (1967).

9. In the three-dimensional case, we add series of pyramids to the object to build the surface area.

10. See E. Lorenz, "Large-Scale Motions of the Atmosphere: Circulation," in *Advances in Earth Science* (Cambridge: MIT Press, 1966) for a celebrated application of the concept to weather.

11. Investor interaction is likely to be different if all trades were cleared simultaneously and instantaneously by computer than if they were cleared sequentially over some more lengthy period of time.

12. Option pricing models would seem to be immune to the complexity problems associated with aggregation. However, in many respects, they are much more like The Tool than The Theory. Suppose you are an investor taking positions in the stock and its options. If you input their market prices into the option model, the model provides the expected return to the "tip of the bullet" or the minimum variance portfolio. A binomial or continuous time model (with an assumed variance for the stock) will provide an estimate for the entire bullet.

CHAPTER 13

Final Words

Finance scholars have long embraced the notion that we advance faster and better by *first* creating theories that make predictions about the way the world works. *Next*, we turn to the data to see if the numbers conform to the predictions. If we find that they do not, we either (a) "refine" the theories, by altering the assumptions upon which they are based, or (b) "refine" the empirical tests until the data speak in a voice we can *appreciate and understand.*

The Theory springs from the question: "What would the world look like if we *all* used The Tool?" The origins of The Fantasy stem from (a) initial reports that successive percentage changes in the prices of large stocks appeared to be uncorrelated and (b) an understanding that, if security prices accurately reflected the available information set, changes in the prices should *be* uncorrelated. We spent the next 50 years bending and twisting the data, trying to make them harmonize with the theories.

But most of the major advances in the frontier of human knowledge did not follow an arrow running through the theories into the empirical tests. Rather, *most of our greatest triumphs proceeded in the opposite direction from data to theory.* The arrow goes from straightforward empirical observation to the development of theories that give us the insights *to understand what we have seen.*

In 1887, Michelson and Morley projected beams of light into directions that were different relative to the direction of the earth's orbital velocity. They expected to find that the beam cast *with* the earth's movement would move with greater speed than the beam cast *against*. To their surprise, they found that both moved with exactly the same speed. This empirical result inspired a young physicist named Albert Einstein to reconsider the laws of physics, given that the cosmos is bound by a universal speed limit—the speed of light.

In the 1920s, an astronomer named Edwin P. Hubble spent many years atop Mt. Wilson peering through the 100-inch Hooker reflector. Hubble painstakingly made recordings of the magnitudes of the red shifts in the spectrums of thousands of galaxies. After years of straightforward observations, he drew a generalization. The more distant a galaxy was from the earth, the more its spectrum was shifted to the red. Because the magnitude of the red shift revealed the speed with which an object was moving away from an observer, Hubble drew the inference that the universe must be expanding.[1] Hubble's observations were passed to the astrophysicists. These theorists then crafted models (based on the common principle that the universe emerged in a momentous explosion from a singularity) that arguably stand as the greatest single intellectual advancement in the history of mankind.

From "How does the world work?" to "Why does it work that way?"

We have now seen the results of many straightforward attempts to document the behavior of stock prices. These results do not conform to the predictions of the theories.

They don't even come close.

We in finance: *Did we not embrace our theories too quickly,* before learning how financial markets behave? *Do we not embrace them now too tenaciously,* in the face of growing evidence that our fidelity is unfounded?

Who will now stand to deny the validity of the following statement: *"If, from the beginning, we knew what we know now, neither The Theory nor The Fantasy would have been offered for our serious consideration."* If we agree with this statement, would we not also agree that it is time to discard these long-standing paradigms of Modern Finance?

The proponents of Modern Finance stubbornly stand their ground. In a real sense, their stand is a noble one. They see themselves as standing watch against mystics wanting to take the field of finance down mysterious paths.

But those in power can go too far in their stand against the unfamiliar.

The guardians at the gate should accept the unfamiliar into the arena and then destroy it in fair battle.

Instead, they can look away with disdain and simply ignore—never seriously consider, never cite, never review.

In their *determination*, are they truly blocking a *false* path? Or are they knowingly blocking a path down which the field would forever evolve away from their own formal training and competence?

It's not nice to be *obsolete*.

*   *   *

We have two choices. We can *advance* by accepting radically new approaches to our field to help us understand what we now see in the data. Or we can *go back*, denying what is now readily apparent to most, bending the data through ever more convoluted econometric processes, *until it screams its compliance with our preconceptions.*

In ancient Greece, a scientist named Ptolemy devised a theory that was able to explain the observed movements of the stars and the planets. In Ptolemy's theory, the earth occupied the center of the universe.

The Roman Catholic Church embraced Ptolemy's ideas. After all, if man was made in God's image, why shouldn't he reside at a prestigious place like Universe Center?

But in 1576, Tycho Brahe began the construction of an observatory called the Castle of the Heavens. Brahe observed the movements of the heavens with instruments that were the best of his time. He measured and recorded the positions of 777 stars, and it is said his star positions were never in error by more than one or two minutes of arc.

It became increasingly clear that Brahe's careful observations were inconsistent with Ptolemy's theory. With the support of the Church, mathematicians and scientists labored furiously to create new versions of Ptolemy's model, making it increasingly complicated so it would comply with the latest recorded observations.

In 1600, Giordano Bruno, had been going around Europe advocating against the notion that the earth was the center of everything. Speaking for the notion that the stars were merely suns like our own, he was burned at the stake by those in power who did not accept his beliefs.

Later, Brahe was joined by Johannes Kepler. Kepler had studied the works of an earlier astronomer, Copernicus, and he realized that if he assumed that the earth, together with the rest of the planets, moved around the sun, most of the complications could be removed with one stroke. Kepler realized that in science a straightforward theory is usually more accurate than a more cumbersome one. In breaking with the doctrine of the Church, Kepler was able to develop a more simple theory with much greater predictive power centered on his three laws of planetary motion. His first laws were published in 1609.

That year marked the beginning of the amazing discoveries of Galileo, who began using the newly invented telescope for astronomical observation. Among other things, Galileo found that Jupiter had moons that revolved around *it*. Even more importantly, he found that Venus had *phases* like the moon. *That* could only be consistent with the notion that Venus revolved around the sun and not the earth.

Galileo published his findings in a book written in a popular style involving a conversation between two imaginary philosophers.

The Church did not take well to this. They summoned Galileo to Rome and ordered him to abjure his "false" views.

Aware of the fate of Bruno, Galileo complied and was then forced to live in his home and abandon astronomy.

It is not clear whether any of the true believers in the earth-centered universe were ever persuaded by Copernicus, Bruno, Brahe, Kepler, or Galileo to change their minds. All may have gone to their graves still searching for further, more complicated versions of their model that would make it consistent with the latest empirical observations.

True believers to the last.

*   *   *

May we both spend our final years on the warm sands of Waikiki Beach.
Don't be afraid of the journey to Diamond Head.
You will find it to be a safe and comfortable one.

Note

1. Draw points on a balloon, and then blow it up. From the vantage of any one point, it will appear that all the other points are moving away, and the further away, the faster they will be moving.

GLOSSARY

Behavioral Economic Model A model in which irrational (and rational) behaviors are aggregated to produce a theory of price behavior in an orderly state.

Bottom Fisher Money manager, with no crystal ball, who favors stocks selling at the lowest prices relative to current cash flows.

Chaos Unpredictable turbulence resulting from interaction between particles, bodies, or beings.

Christmas Tree The pattern of mean reversion in earnings growth rates.

Complexity State of behavior lying between order and chaos where behaviors don't lock into place nor dissolve into turbulence.

Crystal Ball Technology (subjective or quantitative) used to assess future prospects.

Diamond Bar Retirement destination for an investor in expensive growth stocks.

Diamond Head Retirement destination for an investor in cheap value stocks.

Error-Driven Volatility Stock volatility induced by over and under reactions of stock prices to real economic events.

Event-Driven Volatility Stock volatility induced by instantaneous and unbiased market price reactions to real economic events.

The Fantasy Belief that stock prices always adjust to reflect the appearance of new and relevant information in an instantaneous and un-biased manner.

Fossil A piece of evidence that contradicts the efficient market hypothesis.

GO The golden opportunity to go to Diamond Head rather than Diamond Bar.

Great Hall of Divine Saviors Shrine dedicated to the worship of preposterous interpretations of evidence contradicting the efficient market hypothesis.

Growth Stock A stock selling at an expensive price relative to current cash flow, earnings, dividends and book value and for which earnings per share might be expected to grow at a faster than average rate for a relatively short time into the future.

Growth Train #1 Revision in standards for valuing stocks that occurred in the late 1920s.

Growth Train #2 Revision in standards for valuing stocks that occurred in the early 1960s.

Heretic A true disbeliever in The Theory and The Fantasy.

Holy Temple of Efficient Markets Building located at 1101 E. 58th St., Chicago, Illinois.

Hot Shots Believers, in the late 1920s, in the new standards for valuing growth stocks.

Implied Volatility The market's assessment of its volatility given by the prices of options on the market index.

Market Beta Sensitivity of an individual stock's return to changes in the aggregate market return.

New Finance Belief that conclusions about the nature of pricing in financial markets should be based on straightforward empirical estimation rather than theoretical constructs that aggregate from individual behaviors.

Old Timers Nonbelievers, in the late 1920s, in the new standards for growth stock investing.

Price-Driven Volatility Stock volatility induced largely by reaction to changes in the market's estimate of its volatility.

Rational Economic Model Model in which rational behaviors are aggregated to produce a theory of price behavior in an orderly state.

Real Information Set Any information relevant to the pricing of stocks other than the stock price history.

Rodeo Driver Fictitious money manager, with no crystal ball, who favors stocks selling at the highest prices relative to current cash flows.

Student *T*-Statistic Mean value divided by its standard error.

The Theory (alias CAPM, SLM, SLB, SLFB, etc.) Belief that *all* investors hold portfolios that have mean-variance properties consistent with those found with The Tool.

The Tool Procedure to find the portfolios with the lowest possible volatility of return given an objective for expected return.

Value Stock A stock selling at a cheap price relative to cash flow, earnings, dividends and book value, and for which earnings per share might be expected to grow at a slower than average rate for a relatively short time in the future.

Zealot A true believer in The Theory or The Fantasy, or both.